So Brief a Dream

So Brief a Dream

Rafaelle, Duchess of Leinster

Foreword by Beverley Nichols

W. H. Allen
London and New York
A division of Howard & Wyndham Ltd
1973

PRINTED AND BOUND IN GREAT BRITAIN BY BUTLER AND TANNER LTD,

FROME AND LONDON, FOR THE PUBLISHERS,

W. H. ALLEN & CO. LTD, 43 ESSEX STREET, LONDON WC2R 3JG.

ISBN 0491 01290 X

To My Mother

With grateful thanks to
Barbara Cartland for
believing in my story
and to Hugh Corbett-Palmer
for believing that I could write it
and to Beverley Nichols for
believing in me.

A section of illustrations follows
page 96

Foreword

BEVERLEY NICHOLS

The operative word in this book is the word 'duchess'. To say this is not to suggest that Rafaelle Leinster is more of a snob than the rest of us; on the contrary. To her, the word always had a fairy-tale quality, and the position it carried, a magic of its own. Anybody with a grain of poetry in his make-up will agree with her. After all, the heroine of Webster's masterpiece would lose much of her immortal lustre if she trod the world's stages as Mrs Malfi; and the legend of the Princess and the Pea would arouse small sympathy if the lady who was troubled by this tiresome vegetable had been called Mrs Smith.

Rafaelle, throughout the long years of our friendship, has often reminded me of the Princess and the Pea. There have been moments when shadows have passed over her face that I have been unable to interpret, when there has been a glint of fear in her eyes for which there was no apparent reason. In the present book, this malaise may not always be apparent, if it is read as a common-or-garden success story. (Not that it is a success story.) But it lingers, between the lines.

Turn back the clock to the twenties. Set the scene, at midnight, in a shabby little house in Pimlico where a young man is writing words, which, he hopes, some editor will purchase one of these days. There is a knock on the door, and when it is opened, a young woman is revealed. She is of luminous beauty, and when she speaks she seems to be out of breath, as though she had been running away from something, or somebody.

'Beverley, may I use your telephone?'

The request is unexpected, at this time of night, but of course she can use it. I take her into the study.

'It's to New York,' she says. 'And I'm afraid it's rather private.'

7

I leave her alone, closing the door behind me. I do not need to be told the name of the man to whom she is speaking. Well—if he makes her happy, that's all that matters.

When she comes out she looks radiant. She fumbles in her bag and pays for the call. Rafaelle always pays her debts. Sometimes, I fancy, she overpays them.

The honeymoon of this strange bitter-sweet alliance was spent at my cottage in Huntingdonshire, which some readers of the older generation may remember as the setting for a book called *Down the Garden Path.** It was an interlude of enchantment, with precisely the required ingredients of the best fairy-tales. The sun shone, the roses laughed through .the windows, the garden was heavy with the scent of wall-flowers, and if there was not a nightingale, there should have been. She wrote me only one letter from the cottage and I remember only one phrase of it . . . 'I am walking to the sound of music'. This, from her, was an indication of supreme happiness. She has always been deeply affected by music. Years later, Malcolm Sargent, who was her devoted friend, said . . . 'I can always tell if Rafaelle is in front when I'm playing; she seems to give a special intensity to the whole audience.'

The music of those early days did not endure. How could it have done? It is not my business to apportion praise or blame, but I think that even Leinster would agree that there were occasions when he was not, perhaps, very easy to understand. My contacts with him were few, but they remain vividly in my memory. One of them was at an enormously expensive dinner party in the New York Ritz. It was given in his honour by a somewhat rococo financier, and none of us had any idea why we had been bidden. At the end of it Leinster rose to his feet and made a delightful speech about nothing at all. The financier looked pained. Evidently Leinster had not come up to scratch. He had been expected to act as a distinguished figure-head for a new sort of wrist watch, which was supposed to go for ever,

* Now condensed with two of my other books in *The Gift of a Garden*, W. H. Allen, 1971.

without being wound up. Leinster had not even mentioned the watch. However, we did not complain, for at the end of the party each of us was presented with one of the watches, chastely designed and mounted.

Years later, at a sun-baked luncheon party in the South of France, when Rafaelle was no longer the reigning duchess, and when a great deal of very turbulent water had flowed under a great many social bridges, Leinster—whose guest I was—came up to me and said . . .

'Beverley, have you still got that watch I gave you? Yes? And did it never stop?'

'No,' I answered, 'it never stopped.'

He looked as delighted as a schoolboy who had just won a race. But only for a moment, for I was obliged to add . . .

'It never stopped. Because it never started.'

Which was quite true. The glittering trophy I had taken from the Ritz was a dud. Eighteen carat gold, wrapped in the delicate satin ribbons, but inert. Lifeless and meaningless.

If one were trying to be clever, and seeking for artful analogies, one might suggest that this curious bauble was in some way symbolic of the relationship which is described in the following pages. 'Never stopped, never started. Inert. Lifeless, meaningless.' But that would be grossly unfair to both parties. The relationship did indeed start, to the sound of music. It was never lifeless or meaningless, because Rafaelle has always been vibrantly alive, and even if she has not always been quite sure of what she meant, she has always meant *something*, which is more than can be said of some of one's dearest girl-friends.

Perhaps the whole tangle is best resolved if we remember that this is really the chronicle of a fairy-tale that failed. The story had all the classical ingredients. There was youth, there was beauty; there was pageantry and pomp; there was a gallant lover—Leinster was a very courageous man—and an adorable bride; there was the crowded choreography of the aristocratic entourage and the not-so-aristocratic hangers-on. But something went wrong with the script. The cast forgot their roles. The

9

orchestra faltered, the conductor laid down his baton, and Rafaelle was left alone, on an empty stage.

The moral of it all? I suppose we could sum it up by suggesting that young ladies, particularly beautiful young ladies from America, should never believe in fairy-tales. This was Rafaelle's weakness . . . or was it maybe her strength? I wouldn't know. All I can say is that in spite of the passage of the years she is still beautiful, and there is still the gleam of the rainbow in her eyes. Rainbows are difficult to put on paper, and in these pages they may not be imprisoned in immortal prose. But they are there, if you read between the lines.

Chapter 1

I was born in a big brass bed in Brooklyn, just before Christmas, in a howling gale, at seven o'clock at night. Within the hour— my mother told me—my father stood at the foot of the bed, beating his fist on the rail, shouting, 'Damn it, the soup is cold!' I should have known then how it would be, but one is not exactly 'with it' at ten minutes old. How could I know that my father would beat the air, my mother always win, and that my mop of curls would one day wear a coronet that hurt and was badly tarnished—and make it shine!

My mother never stopped reminding me that my birth caused her the 'pangs of Hell' and that I must be spared such agony. I was—I never had my babe. My father, Robert Davidson Kennedy, born of parents from the Irish hills of Derry, was tall, dark and very handsome, a perfectionist with a sense of neatness, order and elegance inherited by his daughter. He had a pitiful need for self-importance which my mother denied him. His charm and good looks caught my mother's fancy and he, seeing a tiny exquisite creature with a skin like rose petals and hair of gold, was captured. With a father who lived in a fine house, who drove a pair of high-stepping horses, with an English coachman named Symes, who sat with arms folded at the back of the phaeton, wearing livery, high boots and a cockaded hat . . . well, why not?

The earliest thing I can remember about me was falling down on a path in the garden of my grandfather's house in Brooklyn and cutting my knee. I think I made quite a fuss! I don't remember my grandmama, whose parents came from Essex, at all, but my grandfather I remember very well indeed. He too was small and cocky and dapper, with his grey spats, flower in his buttonhole and a wonderful gold watch that chimed. Having peddled newspapers in his bare feet on trains, he was very proud of having made a modest fortune all on his own, and of his success, which he wore with style and great generosity. My grandpapa, Andrew Jackson Nutting, cut quite a figure, and was known as the Little Colonel. Why, I never knew, but to me he was a General, and I loved him and he loved me . . . the only really unselfish love I ever knew.

There was little sweetness between my mother and father, and I was soon smuggled away by my mother, with my nurse, to a pretty town in Connecticut. It was called Ridgefield, and there was a long wide avenue of wonderful trees running beside our house. My mother divorced my father, which led to the dreaded visits I was obliged to make several times a year to see him.

I never knew my father as a father, only as an aggressive, desperate, alarming man who used to beat his fist on the table in a crowded restaurant till the glasses and silver jangled, shouting, 'Do you love your father?' This always frightened me so much that I would run crying from the room. Indeed it upset me so seriously that the meetings had to become less and less frequent, for I became sick even at the thought of going to see him. How they wanted to possess me, these two, but my poor father hadn't a chance! My mother had endured 'pangs of Hell' to give me my life, and she was jolly well going to live it—and has.

I was brought up to fear and to shine, but with no sense of real values. I never knew cosiness, self-control, discipline or the natural joy of living and loving except with animals. There was my small world of communion and the aloneness that became mine for keeps. I lived Life only in theory, unsure of my welcome among people. I was highly strung and never allowed to forget that I was delicate. Consequently I had to sleep out-of-doors even in winter under a featherbed, and would wake up in the morning to find my bed covered with drifts of snow, which I thought rather exciting, and I have loved the snow ever since. How I hated that disgusting carrot juice with which my wretched nurse chased me to pour down my throat! Every time I see a carrot I pass it with a rush, remembering those awful gallops round the garden of long, long ago.

I was very thin, and once, when I longed for affection and to be cuddled, I crawled into my mother's bed. 'You have bony knees,' she said to me. 'They stick into me. Go away!' I am sure she was right. I went away. I never tried to get into her bed again, for after that we moved to New Canaan, and, even if I had wanted her affection, I found that her door was always locked.

Happily for me, she bought several Shetland ponies to breed because she was bored. How I loved those ponies! I rode them, trained them and fed them. They were my happiness. I also had a small lamb that I raised on a bottle; he always followed me around when I walked, or ran behind my pony when I rode, sometimes for miles, in the woods and fields.

I had three favourite ponies: Daisy, a little calico brown and white wall-eyed sweetie; Mischief, who was black and white, and deserved her name, for she kicked everyone but me; and Domino, a beautiful little black stallion with one white foreleg. He foaled my Daisy, and Mischief kicked her—and killed her and her unborn foal just as it was being born. Such a terrible thing should never have been allowed to happen, but my mother really did not care much about the ponies after she had got them, so that they had, alas, been left together in a field, all five of them—and then there were only four. I will never forget my beloved Daisy dying. She made such pitiful little whimpering noises for me to come into her stall where she lay in agony, and tried to nuzzle me when I sat weeping, holding her lovely head in my arms until she could nuzzle no more. I have never forgotten that unnecessary suffering and sadness. I was only a little girl; it was my first big pain and somehow a warning.

In this New Canaan I also learned fear. I had no sisters or brothers, so my mother was everything to me, and whatever she told me I believed. Whenever there was a thunderstorm coming she would wake me up in the night and take me quickly downstairs into a cupboard under the stairs, to hide from the flashes and bangs. She would put me in rubber boots and seat me on a featherbed, telling me that they were non-conductors of lightning and would protect me if the house were struck. I would sit there holding my ears, crying, and shaking with fright, until the storm had passed. Such things one never gets over, and reason has no effect. It is just the same today.

One moonless night, when my mother was taken ill and the doctor was called, I was told that he must hurry or she might not live until dawn. I remember running out into the avenue in front of our house to watch for the doctor, gibbering with terror, and jumping up and down, sobbing and crying, 'Please God, hold back the dawn . . . hold back the dawn . . . don't take my mother away.' My mother quickly recovered, and soon after married again—a poor local young man who smashed his car into a telegraph pole, was crippled for life, and that soon finished that.

My mother sold the house, my adorable ponies, and Poppy, the Jersey cow, and off we moved to Stamford, where she soon found another nice, ineffectual man and married him. All her husbands had looks but no dollars, and they bent to her will.

We then moved to Shippan Point where we settled in a pretty white house, and I went to school for the first time. I was entered as a day pupil in the Misses Low and Hayward's Boarding School for Girls—very grand, and only for girls from what were called 'the best families' in the country. I am sure they were, but never having known many girls, or much discipline, I resented everything and consequently learned virtually nothing at all. All I remember is wearing a ghastly middy blouse and serge bloomers, and tearing round a hockey field, bows, buck teeth and all, waving my stick in the air to the terror of everyone. The only people I remember well were Miss Crossman, the headmistress, who was kind to skinny, jumpy me, and the two Mellon girls, who sat behind me in the schoolroom. Dark-eyed handsome Margaret was the daughter of Paul Mellon, who gave Washington that wonderful gallery, and vague, fair-haired Ailsa was her cousin, who was always late for classes, and could never get her cufflinks to work, or her hair either. Ailsa married, as his first wife, David Bruce, who became the American ambassador in London. I liked these girls, and we used to enjoy classes together, but they came from far away, and in time, alas, I lost them.

As I grew older, I was allowed to drive a car—a green Stutz Bearcat. I thought I was the cat's whiskers, and drove every time I got the chance. After all, hadn't I been taught to do just that? I used to take my stepfather to the station in the morning, and collect him at night. Sometimes in the morning on my way back, I would see Clare Booth waiting at the trolley stop and give her a lift. She was fat and pretty then, very shy and grateful to be smiled upon. I have always thought her a beautiful creature, and watched her leave her rather lonely life in Stamford and marry rich, social George Brokaw of New York. She became slim, elegant, even more beautiful, a personality, and the mother of one daughter. Her shyness left her, and cleverness became her well. She wrote plays and entered the world of words and caustic wit. She parted from Brokaw, married Henry Luce, went into politics, and campaigned for the President. She then became America's first ambassadress in Rome. Unhappily, I lost touch with this brilliant, gentle (yes, gentle) friend of long ago, but I have always followed her career with proud and affectionate interest.

I had learned virtually nothing in school, and precious little out of it, so it did not really matter when we packed up and left the little white house in Shippan Point. Mother had married yet again! A kindly, gentle, inarticulate, simple man, who lived long enough to love her—and die; rejected and alone, far away on a farm in Pennsylvania.

We moved to Greenwich into another white house. Then again, into an ugly affair that squatted well back from Putnam Hill, up which, or down which General Putnam galloped to victory—whoever General Putnam was. Anyway, there was a barn for my tall chestnut police horse, who loved wild strawberries, and for my lovely black labrador, Holly. He always followed me when I drove in my sleigh in the snow, and was at my heels when I rode for miles in the sunny months and the glorious autumn . . . just as my lamb had followed me as a child.

There was also room for Emma and Ples, the coloured couple who loved to cook, laugh and sing—and what music it was! Emma, as wide as she was high, and Ples (short for Pleasant), slim and handsome, with a voice like an organ. He used to play a zither in the kitchen where I would join them while they sang spirituals from the heart, and with the heart.

Why we went to Greenwich I don't know, unless my mother wanted to be near her father and sister, my Aunt Agnes, which brought no joy to any of them. My Aunt Agnes loved flowers, wore a wig, and adored the man she married; he was a sex maniac and, believe it or not, she never knew! Her garden was her life, and people came from near and far to see it, for it was a dream of beauty—indeed the only beauty and happiness she ever had. My grandfather lived in a fine house in Belle Haven, named 'Casa Mia'. Every Christmas all the family would gather there to feast, and were obliged afterwards to sit and watch Baby (that's me) dance barefoot in a yard of cheesecloth to 'The Storm' from *William Tell*. Of course I had to steal everyone's thunder, so thunder it was. How else could mother score? After all, Baby was grandpa's favourite, and grandpa had the riches! My two poor cousins sat it out year after year, and never laughed once at this pitiful charade . . . and I loved them for it.

Greenwich was and still is a very fashionable place to live. We joined the Indian Harbour Yacht Club, where I trod many measures with many admirers, for I was considered a very good dancer. I also learned to swim—not the easy way, but the only way. I was sitting on the end of the pier swinging my legs and looking down into the deep sea below. A little horror sneaked up behind me and gave me a shove, and down I went and hit the bottom like a stone! Instead of feeling fright or fury, I bounced up like a cork, and swam like a fish. I had to or sink— and I loved it. After that, I never missed a day, come wind come weather, and I swam and swam and swam right away into the smiling face of my first fiancé, Walter Currie, good to look at and good to be with.

When I look back across the years to those happy summers, swimming, dancing and riding together—instead of being alone

16

as had always been my wont—I could wish that I had never left his side, and that he had held me fast for ever, in my own country where I belong. But no a . . . alas I had bigger ideas. Let's go to New York, the sparkling city of promise and success. Walter could wait . . . or could he? He didn't.

I had made a girl friend, Wylodine Jones, from the Middle West with a million-dollar smile, million-dollar talk, and millions and millions of daddy's bricks in Ohio. Real honest to God bricks that you build houses with. Wylodine also had ideas, so she came too, and off we went to the big city to try our luck. Her young man, Jeff Gaines, could also wait. He didn't either.

My family brought us both together at a big and very smart luncheon of the most fashionable debutantes of the year, at Sherry's. It was a great success, so we were well away. To what? To conquer the world of course, and marry dukes. Well, I did, but Wylodine had more sense, and married a British diplomat, Bryan Wallace, son of Edgar Wallace—the author of the famous whodunits. Bryan was posted to the British Embassy in Madrid, where they still live. They also have an exquisite château in the Dordogne which, I am told, is like a small Versailles, with Wylodine as *châtelaine*, and they lived in great style, not bad from all those bricks that suddenly turned to gold!

And so to New York, where Wylodine and I shared a room in Fourteen East Sixtieth Street, then the fashionable place to live; we thought ourselves very dashing. How noisy the city was after living in the country, but oh! so exciting! Parties, proms, publicity and popularity—all a must for the successful debutante, which of course meant beaux! Here was my first big problem. Being a romantic, and abnormally sensitive and fastidious, I had no wish for sex for sex's sake. To me it meant total possession of the heart—but all I found was total possession of the body. Nor could I understand what men could see in me, and why I always invited a pounce. Wasn't I flat-chested, skinny, self-conscious and shy? Other girls preened themselves like birds, and worked so hard to attract the very performance that I tried to avoid. Why? Surely there must be something wrong with me. Was I puritanical or inhuman perhaps? I had better do something about it. Maybe if I found the right lover I too would swoon with delight. Would I find the heart? Hadn't I been told that the way to a man's heart was in bed? Well, I'd try to find the promised ecstasy in the arms of the great American myth of virility. I tried, and found it not at all. Where was the sweetness of living, the sweetness of belonging? Not in conquest surely? Certainly not for me.

Then I went to a prom at Yale in New Haven. While I was dancing with Walter, I was cut in on by God's gift to women . . . or so he thought. He wasted no time, and whisked me out to look at the moon and into a car for a smoke. I never saw the moon . . . or the smoke. I was flung down and pounced on without a word . . . not even Hello! Happily I had heard that if you kicked a man in the wrong place and hard he would run screaming into the night. I kicked and hard but it was I who ran into the night . . . he couldn't!

Wylodine and I met many people. I met Mrs Ashton de Peyster, who took me up. She asked me to go to Nassau with her as her guest, and a jolly good time we had. We sailed to the Bahamas together in the *Munargo*. We had only three days at sea, but the young purser made the most of it, and we spent the best part of the voyage together, even sitting out on the deck to watch the moon rise and set. When he carried out his ship's officer's duties, I can't imagine. Alice (Mrs de Peyster), thought it all the greatest fun and enjoyed all my romances even more than I did. She too had several admirers and everyone liked her. She was the kindest and the most generous woman I ever knew, not only in heart, but in pocket, with a wonderful sense of fun.

After a doleful parting with the purser, we disembarked and went to stay in great style and comfort at the Victoria Palace Hotel. Alice loved people and was very rich; she never wasted a minute in arranging parties. She knew the Governor and his lady, Sir Harry and Lady Cordeaux, and quite a few other British people who had places there. Every day there was something amusing to do and somewhere exciting to go.

We went to the Porcupine Club to swim. There was a launch from the hotel to take us there and, as it was quite a long hot walk from the pier to the club house, we carried parasols. I loved the little lizards and chameleons that darted across the path. I used to pick up one of the chameleons and wear it on my parasol, and watch it change colour as it enjoyed the ride. Sometimes Alice would hire a launch and make up a party of her own, and off we would go at great speed to a tiny island to picnic and swim. In her very first party was the most dashing young man I had ever met—dark and suntanned, with the kind of good looks that would make any woman catch her breath; so when he smiled on me I could not believe my good fortune.

He was Jack Bouvier, the father of Jacqueline Kennedy. We went often after that happy meeting to swim off the outer islands and, on one occasion, while I was bending over to pull off my bathing suit, something snapped, and I could not move up or down or any way for the pain. I will never forget how kind Jack was to me. He picked me up and carried me to the speedboat and held me in his arms all the way back to the hotel. He carried me up to my room, got the doctor, and nursed me himself for several days, while surrounding me with flowers. He looked such a heart-throb, but he was the kindest and gentlest of men. Back in New York I got to know his red-haired sisters, Maud and Michelle, who were also charming. No wonder Jacqueline Kennedy is the brave and beautiful girl that she is. How could she be otherwise with such an adorable father as Jack Bouvier?

What a wonderful month that was in Nassau with Alice. I met so many British people who enchanted me. They spoke so beautifully, and had such good manners, and a type of quality and breeding the like of which I had never known before; and they were real, not just 'being charming' for the moment, like Americans. My visits to Government House completely won me over to a way of life that I had wanted to become part of. I had to go to England, the home of all this pomp and circumstance. This was in my blood, this was for me. After all, my grandmother was born in Essex and my father in Londonderry, so there must be some natural call from the hills, valleys and meadows of these enchanted isles.

So Brief a Dream

I was thrilled to be invited to stay with the Cordeaux, Lady
Edmonstone and Lady Theodora Davidson when I came to
England. I could hardly wait to get there. My mother, stepfather and I sailed in the *Olympic* in 1924, as American as three
Americans could possibly be—over-dressed, over-anxious, and
overwhelmed. Well, I was—my mother had travelled before.
She turned me out like a plush horse, sat with my good-looking,
obedient stepfather, and watched her daughter shine. I shone
. . . but too brightly. It was a wonderful voyage and experience,
in spite of mother and her doctors' books and pharmacy. After
all, I had never sailed the Atlantic before. Happily, I found I
was, and still am, a good sailor; in fact all of us were. The ship
can stand on her hind legs if she likes and, except for being flung
about and out of my bed with a wallop, as I have been on
several occasions, I rather enjoy a heavy sea. Most people stay
below and one has the ship pretty much to oneself, which adds
excitement to some of the long hours.

On this, my first journey, I wore all the wrong clothes.
Chiffon veils in pastel colours over my hair, and a paste diamond
tiara in it on gala night! A rather premature dress rehearsal for
my life to come, had I but known, but hardly the place to
practise. What a joke I must have looked in my silver lamé dress,
silver slippers with high diamanté heels, and diamonds in my
hair.

Even so, I thoroughly enjoyed myself, and made friends. One
was a Christian Scientist, Charles Tennant, who was a middle-
aged bachelor and was very drawn to me. He had the look in
his eyes of a man who had really touched God. Such simple
implicit trust and faith I have never found again in any man
or woman. Yes, in one, a woman, Catherine McCann, an
American. If there are saints on earth, then Charles and Catherine were two. Charles became the most loyal and devoted
friend to me in England, and alas, paid a terrible price for his
devotion by coming to my rescue when I was married to the
Duke of Leinster.

We all went first to Paris and I visited that beautiful city with
two charming brothers I had met on the boat. We stayed at the

Plaza Athenée on the Champs-Elysées, and did all the things Americans do: drove in *fiacres* in the Bois, went to Montmartre and saw Mistinguett, who had the most expensive legs in the world—surrounded by a nude chorus. We even saw Josephine Baker, the dusky singer, and Maurice Chevalier, whom I thought would have been even more amusing if he had been less crude. Of course, the thing to do was to buy dresses. Even if I did not always know when to wear what, I think I had inherited taste from my parents, who were always beautifully dressed. My dresses were simple and exquisite, even if my jewels were not real; they were at times too much for one so young, but dress sense I did have.

I was fascinated by Paris, but my goal was still London. We booked ourselves onto the *Golden Arrow*, on which we had the most delicious lunch, and on we went to the Channel which was kicking up its heels. I sat on the top deck all the way, so that I would not miss the first glimpse of the white cliffs of Dover. Suddenly there they were, rising steeply out of the sea, and I felt a singing in my heart, and a sense of coming home. I'll never forget that day and our first train journey to London. Those green, green fields and enormous trees, and the horses and cows grazing—surely they had been there always! And the politeness of the stewards and ticket collectors. And Little Titch: he was King of the Boat Trains, and looked after us with care and kindness.

How we tucked into the brown bread and butter and proper hot tea. I was giddy with excitement and joy. We stayed at the small, attractive, very English Stafford Hotel in St James' Place. How old-fashioned it seemed to American eyes, with only a single lift worked by pulling a cable, and jugs and basins in the bedrooms. However, it was comfortable, and we got used to it, and the service was excellent. When I woke up in the morning and rang for my breakfast, a fire was lit in a fireplace in my bedroom and this I loved. Little did I know then that the double-fronted house at the top of the cul-de-sac of St James' Place would be the home of my future aunt and uncle, Viscount and Viscountess D'Abernon, and that here in this very house my wedding breakfast would be held when I married their nephew.

Just like in Paris, we did all the things Americans do when 'seeing the sights': the changing of the guard at the palaces, the Crown Jewels in the Tower of London, excursions by car into the countryside, Hampton Court—the home of grace and favour—to see Lady Theodora Davidson—whom I had met in Nassau—Stratford-upon-Avon, Oxford, Cambridge, and many of the stately homes of England. The more I saw, and the more people I met, the more I loved this little island.

I looked up all the friends I had made in Nassau and made many more. Lady Edmonstone was quite a character. Over-tall, and very thin, she must have been lovely when she was a girl, with her attractive rosebud mouth, which suggested more of a bud than a rose when she was displeased. Even her house in a London square was tall and thin. She lived there with Archie, her husband. Archie had been a courtier, a rather meek one I would think, and his claim to fame was his sister, Mrs Alice Keppel, who had been a favourite of King Edward VII. Archie preferred the company of his sister, who was far from meek, to that of his wife, Ida, who was therefore sometimes left alone. She used to wander about, carrying not one but often three enormous bags filled with I never knew what, and invariably a paper bag with a bun in it, which she would sit down and eat whenever and wherever she might be if she felt hungry—often on a park bench.

The Edmonstones very kindly made arrangements for me to go to Scotland to stay at Duntreath, their 'stately home', where their son Charlie was living with his very rich American wife, who was a Marshall Field from Chicago. Little did I know what I was in for! It was the first time I had ever been to Scotland, and the first time I had ever stayed in a castle. I was welcomed with all the politeness so natural to the British; charming, gracious, kindly and meaningless. Even my hostess had learned the form. Of course I had brought all the wrong clothes, and to this day Beverley Nichols often reminds me of those utterly unsuitable high green heels I wore on that not very happy visit.

I was put into a lovely big room in a wing, far from the bath-room and from the rest of the castle. I felt completely lost in every sense of the word, and rather frightened, so it was the last straw when the maid laid out my beautiful brand new green quilted coat with my nightdress, thinking it was my dressing gown. Hadn't I bought those 'highly unsuitable' smashing green-heeled shoes to go with it? Almost at once I could visualise myself as something of a glorious, gauche American joke, and I wished that I had never come. I longed to go away, but then, they hadn't really asked me themselves. It had been arranged by the mother-in-law and they were stuck with me! Such was my first experience of many to come, of Americans' resentment of other Americans abroad. I did not expect it so I was unable to deal with this unhappy situation, but it put me on my guard, thanks to my hostess at Duntreath.

It was good to return to London, even though I loved Scot-land, or what little I saw of it. It was enough to make me go back and back in the years to come, to wilder and far more beautiful country, and certainly to more friendly and welcoming hearths. But it was time for all good Americans to go home. Walter was waiting, as was our house in Greenwich, and a familiar way of life. Our country where we belonged, our soil where our roots were deep. Then why did I feel the longing to rush back to that 'green and pleasant land'? Was it the song of the blackbird that is silent in America, the haunting wail of the bagpipes, or just the British policemen? It certainly wasn't the grey skies! But back I went, and there I stayed for a lifetime, and met the world, and walked with kings.

Chapter 2

This time we sailed to Europe in the *Majestic*, not quite as over-dressed and over-awed as before, with mother so tiny, so pretty, cracking the whip as usual, and everyone jumping through hoops. We kept to the same pattern and went again to Paris to shop and to 'do' Biarritz, as we had 'done' Venice the time before. In Venice we stayed at the Lido, where one walked a mile in tepid water, while crabs tweaked one's toes, before it was deep enough to swim; I swam right into a bloated and very dead Persian cat. That night I was stung in the mouth by a mosquito, and blew up like the cat, and had to wear a veil for a week. So we went well armed with insect bombs when we eventually went to Biarritz. We stayed at the Hotel California, in the rue de Berri in Paris while choosing my dazzling new dresses, then to Biarritz, where we stayed at the Helianthe, high up on a cliff overlooking the sea and sand. The sand was not quite as fine as the white pepper of the Lido, but there were no stinging things here, except for jelly fish who came bobbing in occasionally in little shoals.

There were great waves to leap about in that were fresh and fun if you knew how to resist the undertow, which was mighty strong. Very self-conscious me, with my long brown hair and come-hither bathing suit, rushed into the sea, and forgot everything for the joy of it. As I dived through a wave, I swam again into another smiling face, as I had done in Greenwich. This time it was an attractive, intense Belgian, Guy de Burlet, who promptly attached himself to me, and set out to woo me and my dollars with obvious speed. So intense was he that he crushed a glass with his hand to show his despair if I even so much as looked at another man. What a mess, and what a bore, but then we were very young, and I suppose he thought that this dramatic bloody act would completely bowl me over. He was my first foreign beau, so I thought this was the way they behaved, and found it rather exciting. Once more, the sun and the sea were the setting for fun and a flirt.

Then Guy took me to a bull fight at San Sebastian. I had never been to one and expected a colourful sight. I got it! Blood and thunder . . . more blood than thunder . . . the perfect follow-up to Guy and his glass. Never, but never, will I forget what I saw and heard. Fanfare of trumpets . . . cheering crowds . . . dashing young matadors with flashing smiles . . . flashing red capes, and flashing knives! Then the picadors on bony horses, carrying long sharp lances. All parading round the arena to cries of '*Olé!*' '*Olé!*' ready to show how brave they were! Then in came the poor terrified little bull, who ran into the middle of the ring only because he had been shooed there. There he stood, dazed and still. But he had to be fierce, he had to be, so the matadors rushed at him, flapping their red capes in his face, and sticking knives in his head, and the picadors rode round him, poking him with their lances, to make him attack. Poor little wretch, he attacked. Well, wouldn't you, with all those knives stuck in your head! Anything to get rid of the pain.

But the horses. Oh God, the horses! I saw the bull rip open the belly of one, which couldn't scream because its cords had been cut, and I wanted to be sick. I prayed that the horse would be shot, but not a chance—it was ridden out of the ring pouring guts, and, believe it or not, sewn up and ridden back again, the same horse! This was not only too much for me, but also for the frenzied little bull, who in stark terror leaped over the wall right into our row of seats. I don't know who was more frightened, the bull or us. All I do know is that we shot like arrows out of that arena.

On our journey back to Paris, while we were in the dining-car, we wanted to shut a window, or I did, as soot was blowing in all over our delicious tender veal, cooked as only the French and the Italians can cook it. The table was for four, and we were three. Suddenly there was the fourth, saying, 'Please can I shut the window for you?' 'Yes, thank you,' said I, looking up into the bespectacled, well-bred, not very handsome face of a young Spaniard. After murder in the bull ring, I didn't feel exactly drawn to Spaniards. However, as he was sitting beside me, we talked and talked and, before we arrived in Paris, he asked mother if he might stay at our hotel and take me to Longchamps to the races. He told us his name, but it was in a new accent, so we didn't take it in until he gave my stepfather his card! El Duque de Conellejos, son of the prime minister of Spain, who was later assassinated. Heavens! a grandee or something! Things were certainly looking up!

I shan't forget my champagne-coloured dress bordered with mink, and orchids for the American girl from my first duke, which he so tenderly pinned on my flat-chested front. We were much photographed together and, when we left for London, where we had taken a house in West Halkin Street, he followed me. I wonder what he saw in me and what has become of him, for he was a serious, intense man, and kissed only my hand when he came to say good-bye on his way home to Spain.

Here we were at last in the land of dreams, in a house of our own in London. Never mind the stairs, the stairs, and more stairs, from basement to roof. Up and down, up and down. No wonder the British are strong—they have to be! And the servants that went with the house. How did they bear it? There was a cook, a parlourmaid and Rhoda the housemaid. Wonderful Rhoda in her crisp spotless uniforms, one day blue, one day pink, with big stiff white aprons and cap by day, and black silk dress with frilly lace apron and cap by night. I adored laughing Rhoda, with cheeks like red apples, who used literally to bend double and rock with laughter. I had often heard of it, but never actually seen it until I saw Rhoda. Backwards and forwards she bent and rocked, with laughter rising from the bottom of her black shiny boots, up and out of the tippy top of her starched cap. It was so contagious that even I learned to rock. Every morning, up all those five flights of stairs, Rhoda would come to clean the grate and light a warm cheering fire for me to wake up to. Then all the way down to the kitchen to fetch my breakfast on an enormous heavy tray for me to enjoy in bed in front of the fire. What a girl, and always smiling like the sun that never shone.

What a difference between servants then and now! Well, there are hardly any now, but in those days it was considered normal for servants to sleep in the basement or under the stairs, according to their rank. The head butler, the head cook and housemaid had the best, such as it was, and the footmen, under-housemaids, kitchen maids and the like, bedded down where they could. And their wages would have shamed a man who shovels snow in America.

The house in West Halkin Street belonged to an American, Mrs Douglas Grant of Moneymusk, who turned out to be a school friend of mother's, much to their mutual surprise. The house was prettily furnished and reflected the charm and delicate appearance of its owner. She was small, with wide lonely eyes, and carried a little round barrel muff in winter. She collected lame dogs, helped lost souls in distant lands, and spent much of her time and money in Switzerland, where not so long ago she died in a tiny room in a hotel overlooking Lake Geneva.

The drawing-room, with its blue taffeta curtains that shimmered in the firelight at five tall windows, was a delight to welcome friends in to tea. Tea was the thing then, brought at five o'clock on a beautiful large silver tray, with silver teapot, sugar basin and hot water kettle with its little flame beneath, and wee silver snuffer to put the flame out with. The china was exquisite Worcester, cups, saucers and small plates for the delicious pieces of brown bread and butter, and slices of fruit cake—heavy, hard and not a patch on our own light fluffy cakes at home. What a load, so beautifully arranged on a tea table, and carried, like everything else, miles up those dark stairs, either by the parlourmaid or by Rhoda. How pleasant it was by the fire, always kept burning brightly, and with the lovely curtains drawn. I had a tortoise-shell Persian kitten who also delighted in those curtains, but only to leap up to try to catch the flicker, reflected from the fire, and swing on them. So she was banished to the small room on the ground floor at the back of the house that became my sitting-room, as my

27

mother and stepfather needed the big drawing-room for themselves.

In this little room, or den as I called it, I received my intense Belgian, Guy de Burlet, my serious Spanish duke, Father Vernon Johnson, an Anglo-Catholic priest, Beverley Nichols, leading author of the 'bright young things' era, and many of the other interesting people I got to know.

Frances Grant, who was very religious, took me one evening to hear Father Vernon preach at St Paul's, Knightsbridge. He was the talk of London, and she told me that the crowd would be enormous, so we must get to the church early. How right she was, the crowd was already tremendous, with a queue a block long. He had a vast following, and when I heard him I understood why. Here was a gifted dedicated priest with conviction, and a magnetic personality that drew people in thousands. He was young too, and good to look at, with a fine warm voice, and style. Frances and he were friends, so she introduced me to him after the service. From that meeting we two became friends, and he would come to see me often in my little back room. When it was cold, as it usually was, Father Vernon would stand with his back to the fire, hike up his long robe, put his hands in the pockets of his tweed knickerbockers underneath and toast his derrière! He was so human, with such a sense of fun, and I thought he was a honey.

Before he went over to Rome and became a Roman Catholic he christened me, at my request (mother had neglected to do so), at St Paul's, Knightsbridge, where I had first met him. An unusual service for a young woman, but so much of my life has been unusual. Frances Grant became my godmother, Admiral Sir Basil Brooke (Comptroller to King George V) my godfather. Clare Van Neck, my future first husband, was also present and so, of course was, my Gyppy—I will tell you more about her later.

'I can never tell you what June 3rd meant to me,' I wrote to my mother, 'as I stood there at the font, wearing the grey dress you like and veil, with Duenna, Clare, Frances and Douglas Grant, and Olave and Basil Brooke. We were waiting for Father Vernon and the Verger, who were kneeling at the altar, wearing their scarlet stoles, to rise and come to christen me. All the while the organ was playing "Abide with Me", which I had asked for, as you love it, and I wanted to feel as close to you, Muddy, as I could, when I was given a name.'

Beverley Nichols' books seemed to speak and answer my thoughts. I felt such a *rapport* with him that I wrote and told him so. Happily for me, this led to a long and treasured friendship that continues to enrich my life. He too used to come often to the little room at the back, and I found him even more charming than his books. Once, when he was expected at Christmas time, he didn't turn up. For our first Christmas away from home, so like all Americans, we bought a holly wreath, tied a big red bow on it, and hung it on the outside of the front door. How American can you get! When Beverley was due, no doorbell rang. What could have happened to him? The next day I received a cautious, tender note from him, saying that he had come, but when he saw the wreath on the door he was so shocked, as to him it meant that someone had died, that he dared not ring the bell, and sadly turned and went away. He was afraid to telephone, in case it was me. The only thing that puzzled him was the gay red bow . . . but perhaps that too was another strange American custom.

When a young American girl comes to England with her family, she is certain to be hunting a husband, with a title of course, and to have plenty of dollars. So the English waste no time in taking her up, and taking all they can get. Of course if you are as 'green' as I was, you fall for their charm, *politesse* and persuasion, thinking, like the mugs we Americans are, that it is for real. Having always thought that I was unlovely, I was naturally pleased when they told me how pretty I was; all of course to get me to sell programmes for charities and parade myself. On one occasion I was dressed as 'Platinum', on another as 'Queen of Hearts', in a wonderful red velvet dress and head-dress designed for me by Cecil Beaton, and yet another, Blue-beard's wife, until I was on every list and committee, and very

29

much written about. The magazine *Sporting and Dramatic*, for instance, wrote:

> *At the first night at the Comedy Theatre, a large emerald green ostrich feather fan made a glorious splash of colour as it lay along the edge of a box, where there sat with Admiral Mark Kerr and his wife, one of the loveliest girls I have ever seen. Her dark, softly waved hair was drawn into a coil in the back. She wore long emerald earrings, and a rope of pearls with a Maltese cross of emeralds, which hung low down against the shimmering white and silver of her gown. With the sweep of green feathers in front of her, and the jewelled green of her outspread wrap as a background, she made such a wonderful picture, and drew all eyes and opera glasses, and there was much interested discussion and inquiry as to her identity. Eventually we discovered that she was Rafaelle Kennedy from America, and I expect it was something of a thrill to make such a sensation in London.*

I was much photographed as 'the lovely American Miss Kennedy', flattered, invited, and just what the English had been waiting for. All those lovely dollars, so let's find her some down and nearly out relation: young Lord Hoodletank for instance, the 'jolly good shot, old boy' cousin, and let her restore the stately home . . . what else are these Americans for? But the joke was really on them, for in this case the dollars were very few. I just looked expensive.

What a magnificent race the British are to look at. Tall and straight, with the bearing of monarchs. Proud of their heritage, proud of their country, and mighty proud of themselves. Nothing can touch the elegance of a beautiful Englishwoman in the evening in her tiara and jewels, nor a handsome guardsman in uniform or white tie and tails, with or without orders or decorations. Nothing that I have seen, anyway, and I have seen them all from all over the world. You watch them with awe and admiration; then they smile. Their teeth! All false, or they jolly well should be! Such a shock to any and all Americans, who care for their teeth like pearls. But the British seldom went to the dentist unless something hurt . . . then yank 'em all out! Even as young as twelve!

Raymond, my first English suitor who asked me to marry him, was only thirty and he had few shining pearls of his own! We met at Christmas time when staying with Lord and Lady Charles Kennedy in Devon, and took to each other at once. He was off to the tall timbers of Canada, and wanted me to go with him. I think I might have done so had I been more adventurous, so I lost a good man, and married another who, to my horror, had TB.

'The Urchin', as I called Raymond, quickly married a lovely English blonde named Marigold, who was full of laughter, and was the right wife for him; they settled in timberland, raised a family, and are still there. I went to their wedding in a small church in Ennismore Gardens; while Raymond waited for his bride, he turned and stared at me, not dropping his eyes even when she came up the aisle and was standing by his side. It was the longest, saddest look I have ever seen, as though he were saying farewell. I broke the look by doing a bolt like streaked lightning right out of the door that his bride had just entered! To this day he still sends me violets as though our spring was still blooming.

Good to look at as the English are, I was more attracted to the Scots and their melancholy lochs, tarns and hills. How wonderful they looked in their kilts and tartans—and the pipers! and the reels! Oh, how I loved the reels! I learned as many as I could, and danced them whenever a kind and patient Scot would claim me as his partner. When I met Lord Carnegie, as he was then, and he presented me to his royal wife Princess Maud, daughter of the Princess Royal and cousin of our present Queen, and they asked me to come to stay in Scotland, I was dizzy with joy. Indeed, there followed eleven of the happiest years of my life.

She was the first royal princess I had met and became my loving friend. What Maudie saw in me I can't imagine, unless it was that I was from a completely free and different world and amused her. What I found in Maudie was a rather pathetic, lonely, childlike quality that touched me, and a need. Something I too had, but I did not know then what it was. Hers was a

need for affection, and to be reminded that she was a royal
princess. A marriage had been arranged for her to the then
Lord Carnegie, an officer in the Scot's Guards, who would succeed to the earldom of Southesk and Kinnaird Castle in Scotland. Poor little Maudie, who suffered from asthma, preferred
the south to the north, but Scotland became her home. Her high
rank did not shine as brightly or as often there as it should.
Once or twice, when I was staying with her and her husband
Charles, I accompanied her unofficially as lady-in-waiting
when she opened fêtes or received guests at functions. It was a
joy to watch her pleasure in performing her royal duties and receiving the inevitable bouquet. She would talk about these
events for days.

I met so many people through Maudie and Charles, for they
took me everywhere with them. I was also in great demand in
London, and danced my way through many seasons and balls.
I'll never forget the ball at which the Prince of Wales was the
royal guest. There was usually a royal guest at a really fashionable ball, and he or she was the star turn of the evening. I was
dancing away with some young man, hoping, like all the other
girls in the room, that the prince would notice me and ask me
to dance. I had on my most eye-catching silver lamé dress,
and my heart was beating like a thunderstorm when I noticed
Basil Brooke (my new godfather), who was in-waiting that evening, coming towards me. He said, 'His Royal Highness has
asked to meet you.' I nearly dropped dead with fright. I made a
low curtsey, and froze. I had been told that one must never
speak first to royalty . . . and HRH seemed to have the same
problem! We tripped and trod all over each other in a ghastly
silence except for 'Sorry!', until he finally said, 'How long will
you be staying here?' 'I leave tomorrow, sir,' I answered.

Hurrah for the biggest clod that ever trod on a future king!
Needless to say, that moment of a lifetime soon ended as His
Royal Highness limped gladly away. What made it all even
harder to bear was that the whole room-full of guests stopped
dancing and withdrew to the sides of the ballroom to watch the
prince and the American girl dancing together. Was it Cinder-

ella? Was it serious? 'Well, you know how he *loves* Americans!' Cameras flashed and people I hardly knew were suddenly all over me. Why? I could have cried. It wasn't even hunt the slipper!

My mother and stepfather went back to New York and took an apartment at Mayfair House in Sixty-Fifth Street, where they lived for many years. I wanted to stay on in England, so mother found me a duenna. Kathleen O'Shea was her name, and she was from Australia, not from Ireland as one would think. She and I took a flat in Rutland Court, and there began the closest relationship of my life. I had always seen her in my dreams, round, pink and dry, sitting on a three-legged stool, and I called her 'My conscience'. She *was* my conscience, and the moment I saw her at Claridge's, where mother was interviewing her, I recognized her and warmed to her at once. She became my confidante, my listener, and taught me so much that I should have learned as a child: such as values and self-control, which I sadly needed. It was a bit late, but better late than never.

What a sense of fun and laughter she had! I have never found her equal. She shared my ups and downs, fears and hopes, and taught me to laugh at myself, which I have never stopped doing. 'Always round the corners and leave no sharp edges,' she told me, and: 'Believe everyone honest, but trust no one.' I have tried to live by these ever since, for how right she was, my pretty Gyppy, with her beautiful wavy grey hair and steadfast blue eyes that saw all, knew all and heard all. She was as wise as the little brown owl that, so many years later, sits on my windowsill in Grosvenor Square, and cries when the moon rises high. I tip my hat and smile.

Gyp and I loved the little flat where many friends used to come: Maudie and Charles, Lady Edmonstone, the Mark Kerrs who wanted to take me under their wing, American beaux, British beaux. Then we decided to go for a swim in the sea—my usual wish every summer. So we went back to Biarritz, and again to the Helianthe. Heaven help us, who should be arriving that night in the suite next to ours but the Prince of Wales, and his brother, Prince George! I was shown his rooms filled with flowers and wished that I had made a more favourable impression at the ball in London. They stayed only a couple of days at the Helianthe on their way to Spain, but the Prince of Wales saw me at the casino and asked if I were Miss Kennedy. To my great surprise and delight, he sent me all his flowers when he left, with a message of regret that we had not met again. That made my day, my night, and my future a richer thing.

Another journey we took was in the winter. Gyp loved to skate, and I to ski, so off we went to Pontresina to slide down hills and have fun. Have fun we did, for we met Mrs Lionel Whitefoord, her son Alan, and his tutor, Eric Keown, who later became editor of *Punch*. Eric was six feet seven inches tall, and for some reason or other I called him 'The Czar', and he called me 'Czarina', and we laughed all and every day, and as much of the nights as we could keep awake. Being out skiing all day makes you tired and sleepy, and as Alan had a touch of TB none of us stayed up late on our *Kurhaus*; but we danced to the oompha, oompha Swiss German band in the evenings, and slid down hills on skis, sleighs and trays by day.

When I think how I used to go over to St Moritz to watch the horse races on ice, and ski back over the mountain to Pontresina by moonlight all alone, I can't believe it was me. But it was, and one still, freezing night I fell and one leg went north and the other south, and the tears spurted from my eyes with pain; yet the fear was worse than the pain, for I knew if I didn't get up and go, I would still be there, frozen to that icy patch . . . and never have worn a crown, except in heaven!

Gyp and I became such friends with Memo and Alan Whitefoord that we visited them in the summer at Lord Rothermere's villa, La Dragonnère, in the South of France. What a villa it was and in such grand style, or so it seemed to me, for I had never stayed in one before. I hardly dared to move in my bed it was so beautiful, and those white fur rugs spread on the floor on either side—dare one step on them? I'd try, but first I had to brave and ring for one of the countless servants to bring me my breakfast. I hoped that I matched the room in my pretty nightie and bed-jacket. It was like a fairy tale, and I was full of it, and wished that it would never end. But it was just another of hundreds of episodes. Lord Rothermere was Alan's godfather, and lent him his villa to get well in, though Alan, alas, was marked to die young. He was as handsome as he was irritable and moody—typical characteristics of TB, as I was to learn later when I married my first husband.

It was not in London that I met my first husband, but in Scotland, where we were both staying with a bachelor millionaire and his sister who had taken a moor for grouse shooting. Our host was Stanley Bond, who was very generous to charities, and kind to minor royalties. He hoped to receive a knighthood, which he eventually did. I met him in London, where he lived, and he used to whirl me round in his grey Rolls-Royce and send me dozens and dozens of roses. When he took the lodge in Braemar he whirled me up there, right into the arms of auburn-haired, handsome Clare Van Neck.

Clare had had a rough time in the war which left him with a stiff bent arm from wounds, and TB. He wore his clothes well, as all Englishmen do, usually brown tweeds to set off his colouring. He was considered a good shot, in spite of his handicap. There is no better *entrée* to countless invitations the year round for a man than to be a 'jolly good shot, old boy'. He used to take me with him into his butt, and in the evenings in the big billiard room in the lodge where we gathered after dinner for coffee, liqueurs and talk, he watched me all the time. He called me 'little lady' and fell for me hard . . . well, as hard as any Englishman can fall for anyone, which is never beyond the 'done thing'. Of course Clare had no job; that was not for the gentry, even though his brother, Stephen, was Chief Constable of Norfolk . . . but that was different. Nor, of course, did he have any money except his war hero's pension. He also had TB, from which he told me he had fully recovered; no one else told me anything at all.

We had decided to celebrate my birthday together, Clare and I, and go to a ball to which we had been invited, and then the telegram came! It was from the Danish Minister and Countess

So Brief a Dream

Ahlefeldt-Laurvig, and read, 'Can you dine with us tomorrow
to meet the Danish Crown Prince, and go to the theatre afterwards?' Could I? Well, watch me! One celebrates one's birthday with a Crown Prince but once in a lifetime and this was
going to be it. Clare could jolly well collect me later and take
me to the ball. We spent the day together, and he left me at tea-
time to rest and dress myself to please His Royal Highness. I
pinned Clare's orchids on my white and gold dress, and arrived
at the legation for an early dinner at seven o'clock . . . at the
wrong door, of course! Never mind, it only added to the excitement, and when I got in the right door, a butler and two
liveried footmen took me to the drawing-room to announce
me. But there was no one there.

Seeing a crackling fire burning, I went over to it, wondering
if I had come on the wrong night. Why was the room empty?
Surely half London should be here on such an occasion? But
no one came, and I stood there alone and very nervous, when
suddenly I heard someone running downstairs. The doors
swung open, and I heard—or did I?—'His Royal Highness',
and in hurried one of the most attractive young men I had ever
seen, full of apologies for keeping me waiting. But who was he?
Could it be . . . had I heard right? I thought it better to err on
the right side than the wrong, so down I sank in a splendid, if
shaky, curtsey. Happily it was the prince, but I was in such a
caffuffle that I said 'sir' too often, wanted to sit down and didn't
dare and, I am sure, did all the wrong things.

Other guests, the Minister and my hostess arrived, plus their
daughter, and we eventually went into dinner; to my delight
and alarm I was placed at the prince's side, and I was only
'Miss Kennedy' then. They all talked Danish, so I was out on a
limb. I think I managed to get an olive down, but my three
wine glasses remained untouched. Dinner, if you can call an
olive dinner, was soon over. The cars were at the door. HRH
took Countess Ahlefeldt-Laurvig with him in the first car, and
I followed with the Minister and his daughter in the second
car. When we arrived at the Palace Theatre to see a musical,
we were shown into the royal box, and all eyes were upon us.

36

There I sat by the prince, the most envied girl in London. I thought of mother and how proud she would be, and of Clare at another theatre with his mother, waiting to collect me, and how lucky I was!

After the play we went to the Savoy for supper and to dance. Prince Frederick seemed restless and danced very little. Then he pulled up his sleeve and showed me why. There on his forearm a running fox had been tattooed. It had been done that morning and he was in pain and wanted to go home. What a funny thing for a future king to do, but as a king can do no wrong, tattoos must be very 'in'. I guess I wasn't very lucky after all—not with royal princes anyway. Before we left, he asked me to dance his favourite tune. The band leader was told the name of the music and he waltzed me round and round, but I could feel him trembling, not because of my presence, alas, but because of the pain and throbbing fever in his arm. He asked for the sheet of music and wrote a message on it and gave it to me. Then he kissed my hand and took his leave as I swept what I hope was the deepest curtsey of my life to the future King of Denmark.

Then I joined my own Prince Charming, and I felt nothing—just nothing at all. However, after chasing grouse over the moors and dancing round London squares for several years, I thought that I had better say 'Yes' to some suitable charmer whom I liked a lot, especially after my gaffes with the princes! After all, I wasn't the heiress they thought and hoped, and had no British training, or any training whatsoever.

So when Clare asked me to be his wife I said 'Yes', and got all the British training there was—and how!

Chapter 3

Mother and Jimmy (my poor obedient stepfather, whose idea of living was his work at the Yale and Towne factory in Stamford, a cigar and meeting the boys at the corner drugstore) came back to London for my wedding. But first we went over to Paris to buy my trousseau and stayed at the Hotel Lancaster in the rue de Berri, an enchanting small hotel just opened by Monsieur Wolf. Such taste, style and comfort, and everything to delight a guest, including M. Wolf and his beautiful wife. It is even more delightful today, and so popular that it is difficult to get a room unless it is booked well in advance.

I looked up my first ambassador, whom I had met when I was first in Paris. He was Myron T. Herrick, American Ambassador to France, a wonderful-looking big man who looked like a shaggy sheepdog. How he adored his orchids. He had hundreds of them planted and growing in the conservatory at the embassy, and spent hours caring for them himself. Whenever we met he pinned one on my dress. He used to collect me in his car to take me for a drive in the Bois, and would suddenly tell the chauffeur to stop so that we could get out and walk. He would tell the chauffeur to 'suiveee' in the most extraordinary American French. The car would 'suiveee' and we would walk and talk; he had recently lost his wife and I think he was a lonely man.

Later on he became very ill and went to the South of France to recuperate. I was there at the time. What a shock it was to see the toll the illness had taken of him! He could not bear to be idle or rest, and prepared to return to Paris. I implored him to wait a little, but his answer was always the same: 'If I stop work I will die.' He went back, but he had to stop work, and, true to his words, he did die and I lost a dear and remarkable friend.

It was always fun looking for the pretty things which are

never hard to find in Paris, especially my wedding dress from Worth, my exquisite lingerie from Boué Soeurs, and that lovely flowing chartreuse chiffon and the emerald cross that hung from pearls. The cross and pearls were paste, but mother's wedding present was a wonderful diamond brooch, all baguette and pear-shaped diamonds from Van Cleef and Arpels, which I still wear with pride today. Indeed, it was my first big jewel.

My heart was more in the shopping, alas, than in the occasion for which my trousseau was being so carefully chosen. I really didn't want to go through with the marriage. Perhaps it was because I was away from Clare, but I was on the point of writing to him and calling the whole thing off when mother reminded me, as she has done so many time in my life, that if you don't like it you can always leave it. To honour a commitment was just a noise to her. One always did only what one wanted to do or did not do what one didn't want to do, the hell with the other fellow. That was the only way I knew, and has proved to be my undoing, for mother always got me out of difficult situations, as I am a moral coward.

So with this easy way in, easy way out, we came back to London and Clare. He and I walked up the aisle of Holy Trinity Brompton on a December morning in 1932 to the altar of doom, 'for better, for worse' . . . mainly for worse! On the day of the wedding, mother, as usual, had a crisis and was going to have the migraine of all migraines and faint or die in the church. Poor Jimmy had to be ready to catch mother if she fell, which she never did . . . not mother! Basil Brooke was going to give me away. His son Bill was my page, my only attendant, and carried my train. Such a beautiful child, like his mother Olave and his very good-looking father, who had all the charm in the world. My bouquet, which I sent to Maudie, who was unable to come owing to the King's illness, was all American orchids and lilies-of-the-valley.

So, with something old, something new and something blue, to the strain of mother about to die in the front row, and strains of 'Here comes the Bride', I walked up that cold, cold aisle on Basil's arm to join Clare in holy matrimony.

They were a wonderful-looking family, the Van Necks. His brother, Stephen, who was best man, and his mother and three sisters were quite something, especially Phoebe, Mrs Oliver Hoare—striking, I think is the word. Clare's side of the church was quite full, but my side looked rather thin, except for the presence of my beloved Gyppy, who made up for all the empty pews. The usual very British reception was held afterwards at 79 Eaton Place, where Clare lived with his mother, who received the guests with my mother, both of them most glamorous in black velvet. There followed the arrival of all the relations, the cutting of the cake and so on. Most of the guests looked as though they had dressed themselves in the drawing-room curtains. Perhaps they had. Then came the moment for the bride to disappear and change into her going-away dress for the honeymoon.

The first night we spent at the little Meurice Hotel in Bury Street before sailing the following day to Madeira. The first night belongs to lovers. I was not in love, but I had married my husband for better, for worse, so we got through it. But I was very young, considerably younger than my husband, so willy-nilly my good spirits returned as we sailed to the island of poinsettias. We stayed at Reid's Hotel. Our rooms were on the ground floor and there, just outside our door and windows, were those giant red Christmas pinwheels growing . . . on Christmas Day!

The first thing I wanted to do was swim. This was not for Clare, who was content to sit in the sun and watch 'little lady' enjoy herself. I had no idea how cold the sea was until I took a running dive right into a deep freeze! I couldn't sink or float or breathe in or out! I congealed into a human icicle . . . never to thaw again. How right Clare was to sit in the sun. Needless to say, I went down the ladder after that, taking the plunge more slowly; nothing keeps me out of the sea for long.

I grew fond of Clare as a husband with time, in spite of the constant reminders of 'It isn't done', which I eventually ceased to take much notice of. He couldn't help it, I suppose, but it didn't exactly make us one. We stayed only about ten days in

Madeira, as it did not agree with Clare, and we continued our honeymoon in Switzerland, which wasn't the same as it had been when I was there before with Gyp. Then we returned to 79 Eaton Place to stay until we could find a house of our own.

Our life in Eaton Place, which I soon thought of as 'dead man's gulch', was run by my beautiful, very British mother-in-law, the servants and the usual topless bottomless stairs. No wonder the British had strong legs and enormous feet. The stairs at 79 were even higher than at Halkin Street. The servants accepted Mrs Clare because she was Mrs Clare. That was the etiquette of the servants' hall, and that is where snobbishness and protocol reign supreme. For instance, the butler, Ryder, who had been with my mother-in-law for over thirty years, gave notice because the new footman had dared to leave the table in the servants' hall before him!

This surely was the original 'not done' house. But no, the servants with all their manners and training, ran England. As they were then, and indeed as they are now, for they are a breed of their own. No common language or understanding exists between servant and master. The only thing they recognize and accept is breeding and authority. They spot you a mile away and handle you accordingly.

My mother-in-law presented me at Court, and there was my first sight of splendour. I wore my wedding pearl tiara, the three Prince of Wales feathers, and a beautiful soft mist blue dress named 'Romance' made for me by Norman Hartnell. It was a lovely thing, all sprinkled with tiny sequins that looked like stars. I couldn't see myself carrying the usual bouquet that would so soon wilt and droop, so I carried an enormous pale pink feather fan. Why pink, I wouldn't know. My mother-in-law looked very handsome indeed, and off we set in a big limousine with a man on the box, for the Palace. This was a new kind of world to me, but I was never as frightened then as I am now. I suppose it was because I was too young, impressionable and excited to be as self-conscious as I have become. It was a magnificent sight in the Throne Room, with Queen Mary on her throne, other members of the royal family standing behind her, including very proud Maudie, and visiting royal princes. Queen Mary took this court alone as the King was ill, but not quite alone, for there, by her throne, stood the most familiar and beloved figure of all—her eldest son, the Prince of Wales, with never a twinkle in his cold—no, not cold, but expressionless—blue eyes, just as they were that evening he asked me to dance several months before. Would he recognize me? One would never know. When Her Majesty bent her head to me as I curtsied, I smiled up at her and him. God help me, I never heard the end of that, for that was just 'not done' and could never be forgiven or forgotten! Oh dear, would I ever fit into this England?

We soon found a little furnished house in Trevor Square in which to begin our married life properly, and I was thrilled to have a place of our own. I also had my first ladies' maid, a French girl, so here was a chance to practise 'how to be a British lady'.

Clare caught colds easily and frequently had to go into the country for him to recover. We would stay with his brother Stephen in Norfolk where he was Chief Constable, or with his sisters Dolly and Letty. I found it more fun in Norfolk as Stephen used to laugh so much while telling a story that everyone else started laughing too, until no one could stop, and the story got lost in helpless laughter. All his staff were policemen and wore the police uniform and looked very smart. Even the butler would laugh so much that whatever he was handing round shook so much that you couldn't take it. And 'Cocky', as Stephen called Clare, who usually never let himself go, became as helpless as the rest of us. But then he thought Stephen was heaven, and if Stephen thought it was all right to roll on the floor with laughter, then let's roll.

Maudie and Charles, bless them, invited us to stay with them in Scotland. The press report read:

Lady Maud Carnegie entertains. Lord and Lady Maud Carnegie have already begun to entertain guests in their charming Scottish home. Mr and Mrs Clare Van Neck have been staying with them. Mrs

So Brief a Dream

Clare Van Neck, a pretty girl who is honoured with Lady Maud's particular friendship, is looking for a country home. Her friends, to whom this information may convey the depressing idea that London is to be robbed entirely of the presence of an attractive and popular member of society, will be glad to know that Captain and Mrs Van Neck hope to spend several months in town each year. She has, like most American women, the gift of showing off her clothes to the best advantage. In a restaurant where I last saw her in London, she was easily the best dressed woman present in a fashionable red coat with hat to match.

Then the so-called colds got really bad and more frequent as winter and the fogs came to stay, and I saw and recognized for the first time the ominous ghastly little bottle Clare had referred to when he asked me to marry him that day in Scotland . . . and well behind a bush in case anyone might see us and guess his honourable intentions!

What a lot I had to learn about everything and everyone! We had found and taken on a long lease an exciting unfurnished house at 101 Cadogan Gardens. It had belonged to Rafael Sabatini, so another Rafaelle came to take his place and live and learn there all about growing up . . . the hard way. There was a huge thirty-foot-high studio with a minstrel's gallery at the back overlooking Cadogan Square. It had old-gold material on the high walls and the tallest green velvet curtains at the tallest windows I ever saw. Opposite the gallery was a big fireplace, and the whole room invited pleasure. I nearly stood on my head with delight. This was for me, for my pianos, for I had two, and friends, fun and parties. Yes, let's live a little, after all that training and coughing in 'dead man's gulch'. What was it, this terrible coughing? TB recurrence I was told, and that nauseating little bottle Clare carried to spit in. O, God, I wanted to be sick or run or both!

Why had no one told me how it would really be? He should never have married a young, spoilt, over-fastidious American girl, or at least he should have been more explicit. And what right had I to marry a man who was an invalid and who needed

43

a nurse more than a wife—and with whom I was not in love!
We couldn't have been more wrong for each other. And that
was when I found that I was expecting a child! I was rushed
to a lung specialist to see if I had contracted the disease from
my husband. I was told that I had and had a spot on my lung;
I must lose the baby, as it would be born predisposed. I felt as
though I had been hit by a bus, for to have to lose the life you
carry is to lose your reason for being a woman.

What a disaster! My Gyp was sent for and came flying from
Malta where she lived with the Stricklands, as she had done
before she came to me. Clare whipped up a winner of an attack
and was packed off to Norfolk. I was given all the pills, sitz
baths and horrors to rid me of the ill-fated babe I dared not
have . . . and once more Gyp and I took to the snows of
Switzerland. There was no child and there was no spot on my
lung—it was a pneumonia scar. When I realized that there
could have been no happy place for a child born with doom
for a legacy and where there was no love at all, I began to
bloom like a rose with my Gyppy to feel natural with. I could
talk like an American and not be told that it sounded like the
servants' hall. We could roll down the main street of Mürren if
we liked, and there was no one to say us nay.

We met Raymond Massey, the great Canadian-born
actor, and his lovely bride Adrienne Allen, also an actress,
who were on their honeymoon. They had with them his son,
Daniel, by a former marriage, a shy timid little boy who is now
one of England's finest actors. We saw a lot of them and
delighted in them, but there were stormy moments. On New
Year's Eve there was a gala dinner and we were at their table.
Suddenly, to my delight, Raymond, who had been down in the
dumps all evening and hadn't even had a single sherry, rose
to his feet beaming and started throwing rolls. First at the
people at the next table, who thought it great fun and promptly
threw them back; then everyone else joined in and you never
saw such a glorious bunfight! Raymond thoroughly enjoyed
himself and ended up singing 'Auld Lang Syne' all by himself—
long before the clock struck twelve.

Having cured all the ills, real and not so real, we returned to London. I had made 101 Cadogan Gardens so pretty, with blue carpet up and down the stairs, and blue taffeta curtains in my bedroom like the ones in the drawing-room at Halkin Street. We had a butler named Silk, who was as expensive as his name, so when Clare took more and more to the country I let the butler go, and Gyp and I enjoyed ourselves eating bread and dripping (how vulgar can you get) at teatime in the enormous green and gold studio.

As I had always played the piano, and often with another pianist in America, I thought it would be fun to do the same in London and make some recordings. I found a professional band leader named Probst, and he came twice a week to play and record—he at one piano, and me at the other. What fun it was! Even Clare and my in-laws enjoyed it, and people would come from far and near to hear us. I can see Maudie now, leaning on the piano and wiggling in time to 'My heart stood still'.

These two-piano performances became so well known that the *Evening Standard* wrote an article about them, and this led to my finding one of the greatest women pianists of our time— Moura Lympany. I received a letter from her mother, who had read the article in the *Evening Standard*, asking if I would give her daughter a hearing if she brought her to play for me. At first I was very wary and decided to make some excuse, but always at the back of my mind is a deep respect for talent and a feeling that it should speak and be heard. So I wrote back to the mother and asked her to bring her daughter to see me. Before you could say knife they were on the doorstep, the anxious mother and a beaming, round-faced fifteen-year-old with pig-tails. What had I let myself in for? Completely unself-conscious, plump little Moura ran up the stairs and into the studio and over to the Steinway, and said, 'What would you like me to play?' Expecting I don't know what, I thought something quiet would be the safest, so I said Debussy. 'All right,' said she, 'I'll play "Footprints in the Snow".' My heart really stood still! The second she touched the keys I caught my breath for the sheer beauty of feeling. How gently the snow fell, how deep it became, and the mystery of the footprints that led to nowhere. This child played with the skill of a man, with all the tenderness and emotion of a woman.

A star was born, and I had been lucky enough to find it even before it rose to shine, brighter than any other, and to give joy to the whole world. This indeed was what I had let myself in for!

I took Moura here and there to play for those who would appreciate her wonderful gift, and she went on and on, playing playing, playing her way to fame. She married a very nice man much older than herself, who tried to manage her—but Moura is not easy to manage. She has a will of her own, and the more successful she became the more she used her will, though not always to her advantage. She had not learned to dress with taste and style, nor to bow, so the little husband called me in to see what I could do about it . . . but I did no good either. Then she parted from him and married a young American.

Even though she lost two babies she never stopped working, and when her second marriage ended in disaster, she went right on playing, for she knew that she has a great gift. Music, in her head, her heart and her soul. She now dresses like a queen, her bow does not improve, but to hear her play is to rise from your seat and shout 'Bravo!'

Clare, owing to his terrible coughs, could take only a little of London at a time . . . and even less of mother, who made him sign a document promising not to take any of my money! Too humiliating, as I didn't have any to take, except what she very kindly gave me. She was so suspicious of people, especially those near her daughter. Clare too thought everyone was up to no good. Clare would bolt whenever she appeared. He, too, was suspicious of people, and one day when we were sitting on a bench in Hyde Park (goodness, how vulgar), a perfectly harmless man passed us who had rubber soles on his shoes, and Clare said, 'You see that man with those rubber soles? Well, he is obviously a burglar, for only burglars wear rubber soles.' And he meant it!

Poor Clare. His health never improved, and he spent most

of his time with his brother in Norfolk. I went on with my life and music in Cadogan Gardens, and went about a lot, but I got homesick and thought I had better go home for a while to look at this marriage of mine—that wasn't much of marriage, at all— from across the sea. We had been married for five years, and no happiness had come of it for either of us, yet Clare still seemed to care deeply. It always seems to happen in life that one person cares more than the other . . . and there is the pain. I had not been to America for seven years, and I wanted to go. I took my Gyppy with me, and Clare came to Southampton to see us sail away. There he stood all alone on the end of the pier and watched us go. How long he stood there I'll never know, but as long as my young eyes could see that solitary figure was there, for he knew that 'Little Lady' would not come back to him.

One day out and I was soon over the sadness of the leave-taking and Gyp and I were well away. She had never been to America and was as excited as a child, and so was I. The land of the free, the home of the brave, the Statue of Liberty was a goddess, the skyline all lit up was paradise. This was the life, and in these high spirits we arrived in the USA.

We went to stay at the Park Chambers in Fifty-Eighth Street. Two small rooms on a sunny corner, and from there a whole new life began. Gyp was always my buffer with mother, whose obsessive possessiveness and chasing cancer drove me up the wall. Having always surrendered to her ego and will, so often found in the very small, I saw for the first time the harm it was doing me, and clung more and more to my Gyp in my longing to be normal.

Not long before I left London I had been asked to a large luncheon at Claridge's given by some Americans for the Duke of Leinster, who was going over to the United States. Not much came of our meeting, except that I liked his fey quality and he never took his eyes off me.

Chapter 4

After we had settled ourselves into our corner, Gyp naturally wanted to see the sights of New York. Believe it or not, one she particularly wanted to see was Child's Restaurant, of all places, where the famous pancakes were made. She had heard about them being flipped into the air by a coloured chef in the window; she wanted to see if this was really true, and if it was to try some. So, soon after we arrived, I suggested that we have breakfast at Child's and over we went to the one that used to be on Fifth Avenue and Fifty-Eighth Street, and sat ourselves down to order griddle cakes and maple syrup. I noticed a rather wistful young man who looked familiar seated with another man in a booth opposite us. The wistful one smiled and came to our table, and then I remembered his well-bred good looks and charming smile.

Of course, it was the Duke of Leinster, whom I had met in London, who had come over to the United States, so the gossip columns had it, to seek, find and marry an heiress.

What a friendly man he was, and what on earth was the likes of him doing in Child's Restaurant having breakfast? Never was there a more unusual setting for the beginning of a romance of a lifetime that made the whole world stand on its hind legs! The next day he invited me to a luncheon being given for him by a Mrs Lardenburg, whom I was told lived alone with her parrot at the Ambassador Hotel on Park Avenue, now a rising glass skyscraper of offices. I accepted with pleasure and went to a very large luncheon of about thirty guests. I noticed several expensive-looking ladies and wondered which one would become the future duchess, and why such an adorable man had to seek an American heiress.

I found out that Leinster had sold his life interest to a professional buyer-upper-of-estates-on-the-rocks, Sir Harry Mallaby-Deeley, for about £67,500 and £1,000 a year voluntary allowance for life. Leinster did not expect to succeed to the dukedom, as he had two elder brothers. Destiny struck swift and hard: Maurice died, and Desmond was killed in action in the First World War. So Edward succeeded to the dukedom in nothing but rank and his voluntary allowance of £1,000 a year from Sir Harry, who had gambled on just such a fluke chance. By so doing he had won himself the Leinster estates and an income of £40,000 a year for the span of Leinster's life!

The amount Sir Harry had paid for the life interest had already been spent, so Leinster was bankrupt! Having become duke, he wanted to buy back his inheritance, but with what? Mallaby-Deeley was anxious to sell at the fantastic sum of £400,000! Leinster was free, having parted from his first wife, May Ethridge, the actress and mother of his son, and was just what every woman was looking for.

Heavens, a young duke on the loose! What more could a woman ask? So why not go to America and find an heiress who would jump at the chance to pay his debts, buy back his life interest, and become Premier Duchess of Ireland! The perfect solution! Mallaby-Deeley encouraged His Grace to do just this, and sent him over to New York to woo and win a fortune— when I happened along, looking for pancakes!

Impressionable me thought this story high adventure, and walked right into it. I had heard that an engagement was pending with a rich woman, and saw a photograph of them together at a race meeting with the usual conclusive caption. There was also talk of his interest in a not very rich girl with whom he played golf. She was very good looking, knew everyone, and I think would have liked to marry Edward.

There were many other hopefuls, but from the day Edward walked me home from that luncheon at the Ambassador, he kept ringing me and seeing me more and more. Within three weeks of our New York meeting he asked me to marry him, high up at the tippy top of the Empire State Building, in the stars! I hadn't a bean, and what's more, he knew it. Such is the stuff that dreams are made of!

All that night I talked it through with Gyp, and the next morning a sad little note came from Edward to tell me of his love but also his terrible fear that his life was too full of sadness and problems for me to take on. He thought it would be unfair to one as untouched by life as I was to be asked to share his unhappy circumstances until he could get things straight and his problems sorted out. I was to think of him as my shining knight on a white charger, who would surely find his way back to me, for he would marry none other. I had hardly finished reading this pathetic little note than there he was at my door, with his arms full of roses!

Naturally he was much in demand socially and nearly always asked if he could bring me with him wherever he went, which was not at all what ambitious hostesses and wealthy widows wanted. Then the press and gossip columns began to write about us, which threw the cat among the pigeons. This was certainly not what Mallaby-Deeley wanted either.

So he completely blew his top and froze all the money until Leinster came to his senses although, bless his heart, he hadn't any sense about money and hooligans. Then I got a telephone call from Leinster, saying, 'I can't meet you for lunch because I am being held by detectives in my room until I pay my bill, and I can't pay it! Will you please come and bring some money?. That did it! I grabbed Gyp, I grabbed my beautiful diamond brooch, and we ran like two scalded cats all the way to the Ambassador Hotel. 'My Imp', as I always called him, was in great trouble. He loved me dearly, needed me, and anything I could do could never be enough.

He was the kindest, most generous man in all the world, with absolutely no sense of money. He was always buying me some little present, and even worried about Gyp being cold and needing a fur coat; he would have gone and bought her one if I had not stopped him. Money just slipped through his hands more quickly than you could count. I can see him now standing with me on the steps of St Patrick's Cathedral, trying to find something in his pockets, and pulling out dollar bills, twenty-dollar bills and hundred-dollar bills like wads of cotton wool. They came tumbling and dropping out all over the steps in his hurry to find whatever it was he was looking for. He stood staring at all those bills crumpled and tied in knots, falling and blowing all over the place like leaves, while I ran round picking them up. Little did I know then that this was to be the story of my life!

But his sweetness and plight warmed my heart and I really believed that I could carry his load and restore him to his rightful place in the sun. How unwordly can one be! I was very young and romantic and believed that, as I had read, 'A king can do no wrong', and 'My Imp' would be king if Ireland were a monarchy. So when the shattering telephone call came I was already lost. He knew that I was no heiress and really believed that I was his salvation. For such loving trust and need my heart was his. Also, being romantics—all three of us: Gyp, Edward and myself—this situation had great dramatic appeal and excitement. I was rushing to his rescue as it were.

When we got to the hotel, I asked to see the manager, who was a most distinguished-looking German. I told him that I had had a telephone call from the duke, telling me that he was unable to pay the bill. I explained that I was going to marry the duke when my divorce was through, and that I could not give him money, but if he would accept my diamond brooch in payment I would gladly give it to him. I held it out and put it into the manager's hand. He looked at it for a long time, saying nothing. Then he took my hand, kissed it and gave the brooch back to me, saying, 'What a beautiful brooch; what a beautiful woman; what a lucky man! No, I cannot accept your generous offer. I would rather let him go.' And he did! Germany may well be proud of such a man whose kindness and generosity one reads about only in fairy tales.

Mallaby-Deeley paid Leinster's bill after a nasty telephone call from Leinster, and he was released. This was on condition that he give me up and proceed with the heiress hunt. But Edward being Edward—the lover, the dreamer always thinking that tomorrow would solve all problems—clung to me with even more tenderness and joy than before.

Then it was Christmas, and I will never forget his sweetness as long as I shall live. When I woke on Christmas morning, my Gyppy came into my room carrying a tiny Christmas tree on a tray. On the end of each branch was fastened a wee gift wrapped in white tissue paper and tied with a red bow. Each gift was a jewel or a charm in diamonds from Cartier designed by Edward himself! Knowing how I loved birds and believed them messengers of good, he had placed on the very top, where the star usually shines, the most lovely gift of all: an exquisite china swallow, which he said he thought I looked like. He must have searched all of New York to find such a perfect piece; I still possess it and will cherish it for ever.

This dear man was full of goodness. Over-generous and the greatest and gentlest gentleman I have ever met or known. Romantic, yes; too trusting, yes; but I was strong, and we had so much in common. Our love of the hills and creatures of the forest, wild places and wild things, the melancholy, the fey and the lonely, and above all music, the language of people and gods, the happiness and sadness of the world, the nearest thing to communication with God that I know of. But there was more to it than that. He was honour bound and committed to seek and find the fortune that could reinstate him to his high place, and I must help him to see this and go through with what he had been financed and sent out to do. I could tell that all was not well, and that he was borrowing money to buy gifts and roses for me.

I was still married to Clare, and even though I wanted to be free, I thought it right for me to leave my beloved 'Imp' to carry on with what he had set out to do, and leave for England. Perhaps if I were not near he would forget me and do what he must. When I told him of my decision, the pain in his eyes made me turn away with grief and shame. How could I wound one so deeply who loved and needed me as he truly did? 'How can you get out of debt and repurchase your life interest if you don't go through with this hideous plan?' I asked. 'I have neither dowry nor dollars, and if you persevere you might just find a lovely lady with both.'

I might as well have talked to myself.

However, he did finally agree to my leaving, on one condition: that I get my divorce from Clare and come back to him! Now I didn't want to leave him any more than he wanted me to leave him, for I adored him and he knew it; but two wrongs never, but never, make a right. So with the heaviest heart in all the world, Gyp and I began to pack; to go away; to leave my love to his destiny.

The pain of the parting was too great, and the interest of the press too dangerous, so Edward did not take us to the ship. Instead, that shy, lonely sad young man climbed to the top of the Empire State Building where not many weeks before he had asked me to be his wife, and stood there watching our ship leave harbour and sail out to sea. He thought that it would be easier alone up there in the sky.

Every day a cable came telling me of his love and longing, and as the days passed I thought I must have been mad to leave such a treasure behind. Wasn't every woman out to get him? And I had willingly risked losing him for good! I grew more and more wretched and wished I could stop the ship and get off. Even the cables didn't reassure me, except for the moment of receiving and reading them. What had I done? What had I done?

Gyp and I sadly returned to 101 Cadogan Gardens. That first night back in my peach-coloured bed in my own pretty blue room, I slept not at all. As the days passed, I tried to pick up where I had left off, but this never works; once you are out of circulation for even a few weeks you are soon forgotten and you have to start all over again.

I saw my sister-in-law, Phoebe, and again discussed my divorcing Clare. With her friendship (which, to my delight, I never lost until she died many years later) and her understanding, I proceeded with the case, which I had put into the lawyer's hands before I had left for America. I had not had the heart to take action while I was abroad. Now I had not the heart for anything or anyone except 'My Imp'. He rang me several times a week imploring me to come back, as Mallaby-Deeley would not let him come home until he had found his rich future duchess. In his heart there dwelt his bride, and I was she, so as soon as I got the decree nisi, I was to come back quick to New York, where he was captive and waiting. Here we must wait together for the decree absolute so that we could be married.

The usual evidence of adultery was produced by poor Clare, and after a few months the case came up and the decree was granted. Gyp and I packed up the house and sent everything into store at Harrods; then back we sailed to the same little corner in the Park Chambers, and the same devoted loving duke, to wait together for our wedding day.

Edward told me about his son Gerald, the Marquess of Kildare, who was a ward of Chancery, and of May Ethridge, the actress mother. It was a sorry tale indeed. He also told me about the sale of his life interest, and more about Mallaby-Deeley and his hold over him. He told me about Carton and the FitzGeralds and his dead mother whom he worshipped. Then he told me about his beautiful Aunt Helen, Viscountess D'Abernon, to whom he had written at length to tell her all about me and his determination to marry me. He felt that she, being his mother's sister, was the nearest thing he had to family, as the FitzGeralds had written him off. He was very fond and proud of his Aunt Helen and Uncle Edgar, Lord D'Abernon, who had been British Ambassador to Germany until the Second World War. Edward was full of rejoicing when Helen responded with warmth, suggesting that she and Uncle Edgar come from Rome, where they lived in a palazzo, and meet us in Paris to arrange the wedding, which should be in England and with all the trimmings. As I was still not completely free and waiting for my decree absolute, it would be easier to plan everything there, where the press would not bother us, for New York was agog and London was waiting to grab us.

Things were getting pretty hot for Edward in New York, so he borrowed some money towards his fare, and I paid the rest in order to give Mallaby-Deeley and his gang the slip. Cables flew back and forth from Rome, and the date was set to meet Helen and Uncle Edgar in Paris at the Ritz Hotel. Without a word to anyone, Gyp, Edward and I sailed away together in the *Statendam* to a new and wonderful life—on a shoestring.

It was on a Saturday night, after a day of high seas with passengers hanging on to ropes and anything they could find to keep from falling, that the waves struck our brave little ship with violence. Most of us were in the lounge, including the captain, trying to stay in our seats while the band played with considerable difficulty. I was sitting on an enormous red plush sofa between the captain and Edward when suddenly the ship shot up on her side with such force and speed that the opposite wall became the floor and the floor the wall! Everything and everyone came crashing into a terrific heap. The piano raced about, violins leapt into the air, tables with heavy marble tops broke loose, chairs, cups, glasses, ash-trays were hurled all over the room, as were many of the passengers. And the captain! He shot off the sofa like an arrow, landing flat on his front on the floor and slid right into the fireplace where my Gyp had ended up! Never did you see anything like it.

The men scrambled to their feet and rushed to pick up other passengers who were scattered all over the place, hurt and injured. It looked like a railway accident. Then the ship swung back with equal force to the other side, and down went everyone again! One man put his foot through the cello; Gyp was sitting on the floor holding her mouth, saying, 'My teeth, my teeth, where are my teeth?' Those near to her tried to find her teeth, which were in her mouth all the time! Edward went to help her, but then a third wave smashed us and he fell and broke his rib. Women screamed, and one was hanging in her chair from an electric light bracket up on the wall! All the time the sea was beating us I quickly curled up my legs and remained in the middle of the big red sofa, hanging on like mad; it tore about the room in every direction, and I was about the only one who escaped unharmed.

When the worst was over and people were picking themselves and each other up in the dark (the lights had blown the first time we were struck) we heard a little whimper, and a very timid woman's voice saying, 'Will somebody please get me down?' Good Lord, there she was, the poor wretched woman, all in black with dark glasses, still hanging on the wall. How ever did she get up there, and stay put?

It was quite a night, but I can't believe that it was a proper tidal wave, or surely we would all have ended at the bottom of the sea. However, it was a night to remember and I am sure that none of us, including the captain, will forget it in a hurry. The lesson we learned was that a ship has to roll over and back three times before she settles, and that the best and safest place to stay is in the middle of a big red sofa—if you can find one—or right where you are.

And so we arrived at Cherbourg, battered and bruised but unnoticed, as Edward had travelled as Mr Edward FitzGerald. He stayed at one hotel and Gyp and I went back again to our favourite Lancaster.

The following day Edward took me to meet his family, or the nearest thing he had to one, for Helen D'Abernon was his mother's sister. She and Uncle Edgar were staying at the Ritz in a charming suite overlooking the Place de la Concorde. I was nervous; strangely enough, so was Edward.

The first person I saw as the door opened was Helen; she took me in her arms and kissed me. Oh, how beautiful she was, like a goddess! And Uncle Edgar, who was seated, was so handsome and distinguished with his white hair and beard. He wore a collar miles too large for him, which fascinated me at once. I had been told that he was not well, and when he asked me to sit by him and took my hand, I noticed how slowly his hand moved and that it shook. There was a book lying where I was to sit, so I picked it up, saying, 'What are you reading?' I could have died when he told me that it was a book about creeping paralysis, his terrible and fatal illness. Trust me never to miss a chance to say or do the tactless thing! What a start to a reunion!

However, as they were highly civilized people, they took it and myself in their stride and overlooked, or at any rate, appeared to overlook, my clumsy remark. Helen was obviously very fond of 'Ed', as she called him, as indeed everyone is who knows him, even if they disapprove of him. I had never seen 'My Imp' so happy and proud, even of me, who had spoken out of turn.

Helen and I were drawn to each other, and from that day forward I spent a good deal of my time with her. I learned a lot about life and the world that I was about to enter; I was not at all equipped for it, for I had run away from school and was not well educated. I was completely out of my depth. Indeed I still am today as I write this story, for after all, that is what it is really all about!

Helen had great beauty, style and exquisite taste. Her touch was magic. I too had a sense of all this, which made me a most willing and grateful pupil, and this was a warm and wonderful link. We stayed for several weeks in Paris, and happy days they were for all of us except Gyppy who would be left alone.

We all went back to London, having made plans in Paris for our wedding. Dear shuffling Uncle Edgar was going to give me away, as I had no family of my own in England then, and Helen, bless her, was going to have a wedding breakfast for us at her lovely house at the top of St James' Place. We had to find a church where we could be married, which was not easy, as Edward was the guilty party in his divorce from May Ethridge, and I too was divorced, even though I was the innocent party. Meanwhile, Gyp and I stayed at the Dorchester Hotel to wait for my decree absolute and the great day. Edward stayed in a flat in Curzon Street and we went about together alone, or often with the D'Abernons.

Beverley Nichols, like a true friend in need, lent me his cottage in Huntingdonshire for several months. From there he wrote *Thatched Cottage** and *Down the Garden Path**. An adorable all-English thatched dream cottage, where I was told mice nested in the roof; they didn't—only happy chirruping birds. It was very old with low ceilings and ancient beams on which you bumped your head going upstairs and coming down; and

* Now condensed in *The Gift of a Garden*, W. H. Allen, 1971.

you bumped it even harder through every door, in spite of Beverley's reminders of tiny artificial flowers hanging from murder corners.

Gyp and I loved it there. I slept in Beverley's 'white room', as he called it, looking down that famous garden path, and delighted in the fragrance of the wallflowers and roses by day, and the big white owl who came at night when the moon rode high, to have its say, then flap its great wings and fly away.

Beverley left us Whoops, his vague and bounding spaniel to look after. He also left us his housekeeper to look after us. Edward stayed nearby at an inn, and on the whole this was a very peaceful and pleasant interlude away from London, creditors and the press.

Back in London I was introduced to other members of Edward's family including his son, Gerald. Poor little chap. He had been brought up to deplore his father by the FitzGeralds at Johnstown Castle in Ireland. Of all the relations that I met, Gerald was the most difficult of all, for I was to become his stepmother. Until I was produced, at my request, Gerald had not seen or heard from his father, except once when he had been ill, for many years. They seemed complete strangers and rather stiff with each other. I certainly had a row to hoe with these two! Perhaps, I thought, some affection would develop when Edward and I had a home of our own and Gerald could feel it was his home also—he had no mother as such and had not seen much of his father. When I met him for the first time he was at a crammer in Surrey. He was slight in figure, not unlike his father to look at, rather shy and shut in himself, and almost my age!

What a wide-eyed fool I must have been. I really believed I would polish the crowns, restore a lost duke to his dukedom, a father to his son, and that we would all live happily ever after. Would I ever grow up?

Soon after we arrived in London from Paris, Edward turned up one morning at the Dorchester in a supercharged Bentley he had bought on hire purchase. It was a dark blue two-seater and went at a terrific speed. We were soon off with a roar and drove day after day all over the British Isles. I don't think there is a single road or lane, rough or smooth that I do not know in England, Scotland, Wales or Ireland. There is nothing I would rather do than be driven in a car. I love it and the feeling of getting away. Edward was a superb driver, but very fast—much too fast for the likes of me—and we often touched 113 miles an hour!

He could not bear any car to pass him. He must be ahead and stay ahead, which was very tiring and frightening indeed. I used to watch any car that was tailing us with apprehension in the mirror and pray that Edward would not see it too. I called them rabbits and dreaded their pulling out to pass, which was just what Edward was waiting for! He would accelerate like mad and the race was on! Quite terrifying, I can tell you but he was a clever driver and safe, I hoped!

We drove up to the Border Country to Netherby, the home of another of his aunts, the late Lady Cynthia Graham. Edward, at that time Lord Edward FitzGerald, had been brought up and spent most of his childhood there, as his mother and father had both died when he was two. He grew up with his cousins, Fergus, now Lord of the manor, and Preston and Daphne Graham, and Netherby was the only home he knew.

From Netherby we drove to Duncombe Park in Yorkshire, the former home of the Ladies Hermione, Helen, Cynthia and Ulrica Duncombe, daughters of the Earl of Feversham. They had been considered the four most beautiful sisters in the world during their lifetime, especially Hermione, Edward's mother.

This is a glorious place, with a beautiful park leading to woodlands, a river full of trout where Edward fished, and a deer forest. When I saw it it had already become a girls' school; it still is today.

We drove over the moors, which were wild and remote. Sometimes we would stop to listen to the wind or the silence. It was here that I first heard the cry of the curlew, surely the most lovely, haunting, lonely sound there is. It touched my heart with a ping.

We would always drive back to London—sometimes four

hundred miles a day—and I would be quite spent and tingling from the vibration and speed. On one occasion I was so exhausted and weak that I had to be carried from the car. But Edward never tired, for he had the nervous energy of a racehorse.

As I have already said, Edward was a shy man, especially with his own kind. The only exception was 'the Priest'. With him he felt completely natural and happy. He had been his tutor, a fantastic character, a lovable rogue, who won the enduring affection and devotion of all his many pupils, usually gay blades and peers of the realm. 'The Priest' was very small and ancient, with an even smaller and equally ancient wife, Marion, whom he bullied, but oh, so kindly. Then there was Burt, the handyman-cum-general factotum and real master of Didbrook vicarage, and indeed of Didbrook itself. The vicarage was a small Cotswold house which rocked with mirth from dawn till dusk and was without a doubt the happiest, most uncomfortable house I have been in—and I have been in plenty of horrors.

'The Priest', known to all as such, although he was the Reverend Allan, adored Edward, and hardly a week passed that we did not drive all that way to Oxford to see him. Sometimes he would come to London, wearing one of his tallest pupil's cast-off overcoats, three sizes too large and trailing on the ground, and always, but always carrying an enormous satchel in which was his pipe, plus sometimes a knitted scarf three yards long! Everyone loved 'the Priest', who knew all Edward's faults and qualities and tried to convince me that I was the best thing that had ever happened to him. He dispelled my misgivings for the time being, for I was terribly aware that I was completely unprepared for the future and the slings and arrows it held for me.

During these hundreds and hundreds of miles of driving, we looked for a place in the country to set down roots after we were married. Edward longed for Scotland; I shared his love for it, but kept on feeling that he belonged in Ireland. After all, he was and still is the premier duke of that timeless, dateless, gentle land, so I steered our course in that direction.

To this day I earnestly believe that had the FitzGeralds been able to give us a small property on or near the Leinster estates, where Edward would have felt welcome and that he really belonged, it would have made all the difference to our marriage and our life together. Old and distinguished families always give a lesser property to a younger son when the eldest son succeeds. In this case, couldn't the family have given us a second place and a second chance? But alas, they couldn't: Edward had sold his life interest, so there was nothing to give.

Time was drawing near for my decree absolute to be granted and our long awaited marriage to take place. The vicar of the Savoy Chapel agreed to marry us in his church, to our delight, and our honeymoon was to be at Carton. Hurrah! It was working. We were going to Ireland and to Edward's home, which alas was no longer his home, for he had fled from an irate American heiress and chosen another American without a dime. However, I saw great promise in our 'return'. What promise I don't know, and to this day I have never found out, but I went on believing in the dream that never was.

Chapter 5

When my decree was announced, the press descended upon us without mercy. Getting up and down to my room in the Dorchester Hotel was a tricky game of hide-and-seek. The nearer the date of our wedding, the more the reporters flocked into the hall, where they would sit it out all day and all night, just to catch a glimpse of the future duchess! More than once I had coffee and sandwiches sent to them, for I felt so sorry for them and their long unrewarding vigil. One actually got up into my room dressed as a plumber, saying he had been sent to mend the bathroom tap. In his tool-kit was a camera, and it took a bit of doing to get him out—without one picture to show for it!

Then at last the most exciting day of my life began to shine through my windows, and shine it really did for once. I rose much too early and dressed myself in my wedding dress. Not white satin and tulle this time, but a soft pearl grey dress and coat trimmed with grey Persian lamb, a small hat to match, grey shoes, grey gloves and the prettiest grey fur handbag. Helen had given me this, and on it was fixed my first coronet, a small silver crown of strawberry leaves. I felt proud, very proud indeed, and I burst out crying! I was a bundle of nerves and Gyp, whom I had to lose, was doing her best to steady me when the telephone rang. Lord D'Abernon had arrived to collect me, I was told; would I come down the service lift and he would meet me in the basement, as the hotel was alive with reporters and photographers.

The ring of the telephone bell had pulled me together with a jerk, so, armed with Edward's ruby and diamond ring, which I had not dared to wear until then to avoid comment, and Helen's tiny symbol of my new and high status, I was ready to face the music. The manager came to take me down the service lift, and dear Uncle Edgar was waiting for me at the service entrance in his Rolls under police escort to get us away to the chapel.

By the time we got there a crowd had already gathered. How the press get to know about things is beyond me, but the harder you try to keep things secret the more they seem to explode in one's face! Perhaps this time the explanation lay in the fact that we had to be married first at the registry office in Caxton Hall, and I believe the press have access to the registry. Anyway, there they were and increasing in numbers like locusts! There was no chance of avoiding them.

It was a wedding in miniature, beautifully arranged by Helen. There was music and flowers, a small gathering of friends and relations, such as Lord and Lady Henry FitzGerald, the cousins from Netherby, Gyp, Marion, and besides them 'the Priest' and the Earl St Aldwyn, another of his pupils, whose hair was almost as white then as it is now, and who had become a devoted and admiring friend. He was our only proper guest, apart from the family. It was not easy for Uncle Edgar to shuffle from the car, up the steps to the chapel and down the aisle to give me away, but he did it with style and, frightened though I was, I was proud and grateful for his arm.

'My Imp' was waiting for me, looking very nervous indeed, with his cousin Fergus by his side acting as best man. This time mother was in America, so I was completely on my own with my new husband and new in-laws. Edward and I knelt to receive the blessing of the Church and he slipped the little gold band on my finger. Suddenly I missed mother and I was very near to tears.

After we had signed the register, followed by Helen, Uncle Edgar, Inez and Uncle Henry FitzGerald, we had to go forth to face the world. But the crowds! Heavens, where had so many people come from? The photographers and reporters nearly knocked us down! Facing the world would be easy after this. How, I wondered, would we ever get away in two pieces to St James' Place for our wedding breakfast. Not being used to having a 'public', I was overwhelmed by the sea of people and cries of 'Ain't she a love', 'God bless the bride!' and the cheering as we drove safely away, thanks to London's wonderful policemen. They really were wonderful, so courteous and calm.

Our entourage with motorcycle police escort made its way through the Strand, along the Mall and into St James' Street, where we turned off at St James' Place to the D'Abernon's house at the top of the cul-de-sac, just across from the little Stafford Hotel where I had stayed on my first visit to England. What a contrast, I thought, as we dismounted from our golden coach and four—or was it only a Rolls?

Our wedding breakfast, given by Helen and Uncle Edgar in their lovely house full of treasures, was both simple and elegant. I was deeply moved and gladdened by their genuine loving welcome to us into the family from which Edward had escaped, as he tried to escape all his life from reality. Perhaps all these good and worldly people who now surrounded us really believed that I had what it took to do what his tailor, Mr Davies, had told me I had already begun to do: 'Lift him out of the depths and restore him to his high place.' I am sure Helen and Uncle Edgar hoped so, even if they had their doubts. They knew how unpredictable their nephew was, and they did not know me at all; whatever they felt, they meant to give me every chance, dollars or no dollars!

My husband was shy among so many of his own kind, yet proud of them and proud of me; so, I asked myself, with a little time and adjustment, how could we fail? The speeches were made and the toast drunk to long life and happiness. We climbed into the Bentley to drive first to Yorkshire, where we had been lent a house by Sir Gervase and Lady Marjorie Beckett, and then to Ireland. Their Graces of Leinster were going home! Off we went, to fond goodbyes and the roar of the supercharged monster, hell for leather as usual. All this sounds so glamorous on paper, as it did on all the posters: 'Daredevil Duke marries American'. And the headlines of the newspapers told the same story, with pictures galore.

We planned to spend our first night together in Broadway at the Lygon Arms, *en route* to our first honeymoon house, as we

So Brief a Dream

had a rendezvous with our wedding presents to each other.
Marden, my new maid, a handsome middle-aged Romany
gypsy, who had been with the Dufferin and Avas in Ireland
before she came to us, had gone ahead by rail to York with our
luggage, so we were free to travel at our lightning pace. Our
gifts to each other were two cocker spaniel puppies, two little
sisters that we had found and bought when we had been at
'the Priest's'. They were being kept for us at the kennels until
they were old enough to leave their mother. One was a grey
roan which we named Heather; the other, which was white
and black, we called Clover. What a pair of little loves. They
were so small they could fit into our pockets.

After our first happy night at the inn, where we stayed as
'Mr and Mrs Edward FitzGerald', we set off the next day to
collect the puppies on our way to Yorkshire. These poor tweakie
little things were put into a wooden box and tied on to the luggage grid at the rear of the car; they must have had a rough,
tumbling, frightening ride. I couldn't bear it, so I got them out
and held them in my lap most of the way. Never was there such
a unique and adorable little pair. They loved us unto death—
their deaths, alas. Heather worshipped 'My Imp', and Clover,
so different from Heather, attached herself to me. So in this way
we let them choose their master and mistress. One should never
ask trusting, loving, dumb little creatures like these two to share
a stormy life; but we didn't know then how it would be any
more than they did.

Heather loved Edward so much that she used to lean against
him, sitting up sometimes for twelve or sixteen hours on his wild
drives from London to North Scotland and back in a day. If he
had to leave her behind, her little face would become as sad and
long as a mile, and she would sit and whimper to herself, while
tears would actually roll down her aristocratic blue-black nose.
She would find a handkerchief or sock of his and nurse it until
his return. My Clover was a jolly, laughing, bubbling clown,
who never missed a chance to get into trouble. She never
worried or cried and would stay put for hours without a sound,
ready to welcome me with shouts of joy whenever I returned.

If a gate was shut, Clover would be sure to get caught in it. If there was a hole in the ground, Clover would be sure to fall into it.

Our first stop after the Lygon Arms and collecting the pups was a most lovely house in Yorkshire. Lady Marjorie Beckett was Edward's aunt and mother of Sim, Earl of Feversham. Marden, my maid, had already installed herself when we arrived with the wee spaniels. Here we stayed for nearly three weeks in a style and comfort to which I certainly was not accustomed. I was 'Your Grace' to all the staff; I learned about protocol and snobbery in the servants' hall, and that our personal servants enjoyed our rank in that holy of holies. My maid went into meals first and sat on the right of the head butler wherever we went. No under servant was allowed to address me or enter my room, even to lay the fire; only the head servants could serve us. Marden was in her glory and ruled them like an empress.

It was a long hard ride to Holyhead, after our quiet happy time in Yorkshire, where we grew very close to each other. The sea crossing was the roughest I have ever known and we had to hang on to each other, the pups, and anything solid throughout the night. Happily we were all good sailors and arrived tired but in good spirits in Dublin.

As soon as I set foot in Ireland I felt I had come home. Strange that, as I had never been there before, but I was a Kennedy and my father and his parents had come from Londonderry. We went to a hotel to tidy up, pull ourselves together and leave the Bentley. We hired a big car, and with Marden on the box next to the chauffeur we set off for Carton full of excitement and in proper style. I could feel Edward's tenseness, and thought, what will I do if he bolts? Thankfully, the high walls of Carton were just ahead with one of the four splendid entrance gates.

This gate was at Maynooth, where the ancient Geraldine fortress castle still stands. It was here that the monkey became the supporter of our coat of arms. The first Earl of Kildare was rescued by a tame monkey during a fire in the castle. The monkey broke its chain and climbed up the wall to lift the baby from his crib and carried him to safety. The monkeys on the coat of arms and crest wear the broken chain. Near the ruins of Maynooth Castle, the Jesuit priests have built a fine college and have brought much good and prosperity to the village and neighbourhood. At Maynooth Gate a small crowd of local people had gathered to greet us. They waved and touched their hats or forelocks, and their friendly faces were beaming with smiles. I knew that Edward was fond of Nesta—Lady Nesta FitzGerald, his father's sister, who lived alone at Carton at Mallaby-Deeley's pleasure. She would be waiting to receive us, I thought, so why was he in such a state? I was relieved when the car passed through that gate into the most glorious park I had ever seen. What had I done to deserve such grandeur!

Pride seemed to replace Edward's fear or panic, or whatever it was that possessed him. Then suddenly he grabbed my hand and shouted to the chauffeur, 'Stop the car!' Good Lord, here we go, I thought, but at least we bolt together. Not a bit of it. All he wanted to do was to walk the mile to the house which we could see in the distance, alone with me so that he could show me the wonders of the place: the lake, the shell cottage—a perfect little jewel made entirely by hand out of thousands of exquisite shells with three rooms in all. Then a sheet of water covered with very rare blue pond lilies and, above all, the American garden full of American shrubs and trees, even a maple! He told the chauffeur and Marden to go on, and we two and the dogs were on our own in the famous Leinster estate that should have been our home.

I hadn't a clue then how like 'My Imp' it was to avoid things. He must have known what awaited us at Carton: Nesta, the mayor, the agent, keepers, tenants and all the indoor and out-door staffs, with a huge pennant which they proudly carried saying 'Welcome Home', and a band ready and waiting to play 'America, my America' for me! Then who drives up in style but Marden, whom they took to be the duchess, much to her confusion and delight I dare say. Hats were raised and they were about to cheer, but where, oh where was the duke? What a fiasco! What a glorious start for the return of the prodigal son and his bride, when they spotted us in the distance coming up the drive on foot!

Some but not all of the people recognized Edward, as he had not been to Carton for many years; but who was the girl trailing behind him with two puppies? Having walked all the way from Maynooth, we finally appeared in their midst hand in hand, after all the pomp and circumstance of the arrival of the new duchess had taken place, with the maid! That was the start of my life with the Geraldines. There must have been at least a hundred people to greet us; they stared hard at me to see what I looked like, but they were quiet and gentle and I warmed to them. Poor Nesta, who looked as though she had just got off her broomstick, did her best to sort out the situation and introduce us properly to our bewildered audience.

Again, no duke! Where had he got to now? There he was, hiding behind a stone pillar on the façade of the house. He had become shy and darted out of sight, leaving me to do the honours by myself. This was too much, but one of us had to say 'Thank you', so I did the best I knew how, saying 'we' when it was only I who stood alone under the huge 'Welcome Home' pennant, holding the little programme of the tunes they were ready to play for our benefit. Almost all were American airs, and when the village band of seven or eight shopkeepers struck up 'Londonderry Air' and 'Home Sweet Home' on their horns and drum, I wanted to howl and join Edward behind the pillar. It was so touching and really unrewarded, for I am sure they thought and hoped I was Lady Bountiful, or at least a Barbara Hutton! That was the moment I grew up with a bang. For now I was a Geraldine and completely out of my depth.

No one stared harder at me than Nesta, who took me in from head to toe in one swift penetrating glance. Nesta was mistress of Carton, and meant to keep it that way if she could. No American outsider would take her place, unless she paid her way and put them all back where they belonged. So better play safe and tread lightly.

Nesta took me to my mother-in-law's rooms and said, 'You are now the lady of the house.' What a laugh! I was never allowed to do anything. They were fine rooms, as all were in this magnificent house; sixty bedrooms, each with traces of past beauty and elegance. The curtains were of the most beautiful silk damask but had not been drawn for years because they were rotten and if touched would fall to the floor as dust. The pictures, however, were a joy to behold. I spent much of my time there, just looking at them with delight. The first one I was shown by Nesta with pride was the portrait in the dining-room of Lord Edward. The first picture I was shown by Edward was a full-length portrait of his mother at the top of the wide stairs. She was really beautiful, standing there all in brown with a black Chow dog by her side. Such a feminine, lovely woman with sweetness in her face. How I wished that she had been standing there alive to take us both in her arms. Edward needed her and so did I. She was my kind of woman, unlike Nesta with her disapproving manner and spinster chill.

Was that why the house held no warmth? Why one's heels rang out down the corridors as one went from room to room? There were no cosy rooms to get inside and away from the world. The only rooms I loved were the wonderful Italian music room, with its organ which I wanted to play the moment I saw it, and a bedroom at the back with a magnificent four-poster bed with a golden crown over it. Here, I was told, visiting kings and queens had slept. Maybe they had brought warmth to it? When I say at the back of the house, perhaps it was considered the front, for I notice that families who live in these places usually live on the opposite side to the one you arrive at. All I can say is that Carton was a glorious un-lived-in, un-loved-in house and held no warmth or welcome for me.

I knew little about the world I had entered, but I realized that in spite of her obvious disapproval of what Edward had done to the family, Nesta was really very fond of him. 'All he has to do is smile, and you forgive him for everything,' she said to me. Didn't we all, for he had all the sweetness and charm in the world. I tried to win the goodwill of this small spinster lady in her crumpled grey flannel suit. She spent most of her time on her grey horse and even looked like one; she shook her head up and down as horses do when she talked. She had an extraordinary way of speaking. 'Yes' was 'M-a-aas', and 'No' was a noise I never did make out.

I used to go out and sit by myself, which is a natural reaction for me, and try to think out the problem, then come back to seek out Nesta to try to discuss it with her. 'I know my limitations only too well,' I told her, 'and would be so grateful if you will help me to help Edward.' She only viewed me with suspicion; she was not interested in me as a human being, seeing me only as an intruder. She told me that she never trusted pretty women. She had had her experience with Edward's mother Hermione, of whom I could see she thoroughly disapproved; she had rejected her from the day she married a Geraldine.

Needless to say, I wasn't told this the day I arrived, but no skeleton stays hidden in a cupboard for ever! Speaking of cupboards, Edward and I spent many dark nights with a candle, rummaging in a secret cupboard he remembered in the old nursery, looking for photographs of his mother. There were boxes of family snapshots; he would go through them with care and stuff his pockets with all he could find of her and tell me as much as he could remember about this aunt or that uncle, but his whole search was for his mother. I don't quite know why, as she died when he was two years old.

Nesta did not know about the night raids, but she did find out about the lovely miniature of his mother with a curl from Edward's hair at the back of the frame. That put the lid on our stay at Carton. At last she had an excuse to drive us away, and wrote to Mallaby-Deeley, we learned later, with whom she was in cahoots in order to remain keeper of the castle, to tell him to cut short our stay as I was up to no good, had no dollars, and had taken the miniature of Hermione!

Before we left, Edward had shown me every path, shrub and tree on the place, and the little graveyard where his mother, father and brothers lay under a widespread, singing willow. In fact, he showed me this during our first hour at Carton. 'Here one day we too will lie side by side,' he said. 'Then we really will have come home!'

The jolliest thing was the ha-ha at the end of the lawns and beginning of the park, where the cattle grazed. I had never heard this word before, and the name pleased me very much as did the perpetual greenness of the grass; it was so different from the hard brown earth or the drifts of snow of winter in America. For it was in December that we came to Carton for those two short weeks, the beginning and end of it all.

Edward's fleeting moments of joy with the place and possessions that he had gambled away were over. He had married for love. So had I. We must build again in another place. The only good thing that came out of our 'homecoming' was that the butler fell for my gypsy maid!

A suitable 'other place' would have been the Dower House, Kilkea, a fairy castle if ever there was one, tiny, with four tall turrets, the oldest inhabited castle in Ireland. Here the Faery Earl is said to come riding on his white charger every seven years for four new silver shoes. You can hear him come and you can hear him go, clop . . . clop . . . clop . . . up and down the stone stairs and away to the glens—if you've an ear for such things. Here too lived the other two FitzGerald maiden aunts, Nesta's sisters, eking out their uneventful days. One did marry, I was told, but no one ever mentioned it.

We were taken over to Kilkea by Nesta, and I fell head over heels in love with this enchanting, enchanted castle, but not with Mabel or Alice, who were as plain as their sister, and watched me through their thick-lensed glasses with concern, wondering what I might do next! They had obviously been briefed by Nesta, and I thought how lucky Cinderella was to have had only two such sisters in her life!

Oh, what I could have made of this place, given half a chance and Helen's taste and guidance! Why couldn't all the aunts live at Carton and give us one of Edward's homes to live in and re-establish himself? To this day I believe it would have been our salvation. But the aunts stayed where they were.

Their hero was Lord Edward FitzGerald, who had led the rebellion for the Irish. His portrait hung in the dining-room—Nesta nearly genuflected in front of it—and had kept Carton a shrine during the Troubles. My own Lord Edward had led his own rebellion against the Geraldines and himself, and stripped the shrine of all its glory. So his portrait will never hang in the dining-room or any other room, except where it now is; in the hall outside the sitting-room of my tiny flat in Grosvenor Square. Yes, he had stripped their altar and tarnished their great name. Naturally, the Geraldines resented what he had done and felt it deeply. So did his young son Gerald, who would succeed him. I saw all this and shared their feelings. I also felt guilty about the riches that I did not have and which could have bought back all that was lost, not only for Edward's enjoyment, but for Gerald's.

What loomed on the horizon was the discovery that Edward was an undischarged bankrupt and therefore he was outside the law! No one told me any of this, thinking, as the British always do, that you know what you don't know at all. All these personal drawbacks and scandals I took in my stride, for I was young and strong in heart and could make something out of nothing, but I was not prepared for the explosive years that followed!

Chapter 6

The creditors had watched our courtship with hope and had even allowed us a brief honeymoon, waiting for the dollars I did not have to show them. Then they struck, and chased us with judgment summonses and the works. I was flung into a world of con men and con women, moneylenders, down and outs and riff raff such as I had read about but never thought to see. The bloom was off the peach, but the American woman can adapt herself better than most and if she has to deal with the underworld she can, and does!

Where could we go—Marden, the dogs and we two? Our flirtation with Carton was over, even if in my heart I felt that we belonged in Ireland. Better go to London, find a lawyer and face the music. So back we went, to the Connaught Hotel, where we stayed for many months. It was and is such a comfortable, old-fashioned, Victorian building. Fashionable, central and just by that tiny green park at the back of Farm Street Church which is called Mount Gardens. I have sat there a thousand times over the years: sometimes to contemplate, to watch the pigeons, or pass the time of day with dear Inez FitzGerald or Edward and many many years later with my mother. It is full of memories and impressions.

Inez was the only member of that side of the family who was fond of me, besides Uncle Henry, who had such sweetness in his face. How cautious they were, these Geraldines, whom I named 'the non-involvers'. But Inez was braver than the others and with her pretty gentle ways we became very close to each other. She became 'family' to me for over thirty years.

There were twin porters at the Connaught, who added charm to the hotel, and who adored 'His Grace', as all the servants did, for he has 'such a way with him'. Several years after we had left, one of the twins died and, before you could say knife, the other followed, for such is the stuff that twins are made of, one is part of t'other.

During this period of our marriage, it wasn't all gloom. Not at all, there were many shining hours. Helen and Uncle Edgar saw to that, for me at any rate. She asked us often to her lovely house in St James' Place and to Stoke D'Abernon, their beautiful home in the country, where I met many famous and distinguished people. But the first excitement was that she wanted to present me at Court. That too was a night to remember!

I had been presented on my first marriage, but that was nothing compared with this. Now I was a duchess being presented by an ambassadress, a personal friend of the King and Queen, with all the entrée and glamour in the world. One's usual escort on these occasions is one's husband, but Edward was not received or accepted at Court, or indeed in many fashionable houses or the House of Lords because he was an undischarged bankrupt. However, Helen was going to see to it that I was. How I wish that I had known then what I know now about life and people. I would have treasured her more and realized the mountains she moved for this American girl to take her sister's place, not only in the world, but, I believe, in her heart. I know that she was an autocrat, haughty and frightening to some, but not to me. We loved each other very much and now that she too has gone, I am very much alone.

The only family heirloom that I was given as a wedding gift was a glorious diamond tiara from Helen. This ornament had belonged to Marie Antoinette. It is all big diamonds in a delicate filigree setting with one large emerald in the top centre —for Ireland, I like to think. The first time I wore it was the night I went to the Palace as the Premier Duchess of Ireland.

Schiaparelli dressed me for my ducal presentation: white satin dress with a long emerald-green velvet train to pick up the emerald in my hair, long white kid gloves, an enormous green feather fan and of course the three white plumes of Wales. Helen was breathtaking; everyone was waiting to see us arrive at the

Palace. We had 'the entrée' and as we approached in her black Rolls with her coronet on the door, a cheer went up from the crowd.

Inside the Palace, hundreds of guests, the Lord Chamberlain and members of the Royal Household were gathered watching for us at the top and bottom of the wide stairs. When we appeared together, there was a hush, for the Viscountess D'Abernon was a famous beauty and I was the first Duchess of Leinster to be seen at Court since my mother-in-law, whose beauty was renowned. The British have an eye for breeding and beauty, so they were curious to see whether I had both. I was so nervous I nearly fell flat on my face as Helen and I climbed those stairs side by side with everyone watching us.

Unlike the first time I was presented, when we had to wait our turn to enter, we were the first in the throne room, for I took precedence over all the ladies. My heart was beating like a drum when the most beautiful Indian Maharajah preceded me, the Maharajah of Jaipur. I forgot everything, even myself, gazing at this young slim prince. He was in gold and white lamé. From his turban with a white aigrette hung a pear-shaped diamond and round his elegant neck were two rows of flawless emeralds the size of shillings; he wore rings on every finger. Never had I seen such a splendid creature and I stood transfixed as he moved ahead of me.

Sir Harry Stonor, who was Gold Stick in Waiting, was obliged to ask me to 'move on', which aroused me from my trance. Her Majesty missed none of this, for there was a twinkle in her eye as she inclined her regal head, heavy with jewels. Surely there never was anyone so small who looked so big, who could wear so many jewels at one time and who looked the queen of all queens. What a pity that my duke had to miss this magnificent spectacle. Never mind, I thought, one day we would win through and be received together.

London seemed the best place to work it all out until we could find a suitable place in the country within our means. We both loved and preferred the country; I felt that once Edward settled his topsy-turvy affairs he would be safer there from whatever the awful temptations were. Then Marden found the bills!

'I think Your Grace should see what I found on top of His Grace's wardrobe,' she said, with her big gypsy eyes full of warning and importance. She had been packing up our things in Edward's dressing-room as we were leaving and spotted them: all bills, unopened bills, twenty or thirty of them. He had placed them there out of sight, out of mind, and forgotten them.

It was very fashionable then to be a duke and duchess, and the Connaught and the Dorchester Hotels were anxious to have us stay with them at nominal rates. They thought it was good publicity and would add to their list of distinguished guests. There was plenty of publicity at all times about us. I took a furnished house in Hertford Street for a short time and then found an unfurnished flat at 82 Portland Place, which became our fortress. I had to sign all documents and leases, as Edward's signature was neither valid nor acceptable because he was an undischarged bankrupt (three times over, another fact I had not known). My good credit in the shops suffered and had to be carried on under my former name of Mrs Van Neck, to enable me to continue my charge accounts. Edward's lack of credit was well known to all, except me!

I am amazed when I look back at how I managed on so little. Edward received a voluntary allowance of £1,200 a year from Mallaby-Deeley which the creditors could not touch. This he gave to me. My mother occasionally gave me gifts of love, which amounted to nearly the same, and on this we lived. Our staff consisted of cook, butler, housemaid, tweenie, chauffeur, lady's maid and part-time secretary. All these I paid, including the rent, living expenses, doctors, dentists, clothes, entertaining and so on. It is only fair to explain that wages then were so low that five servants in England cost little more than the price of a couple in the United States. Rents were modest, but the exchange was five dollars to the pound, and not in my favour.

However, we lived in comparative style and comfort. It was not as grand as other dukes, but I could make a shilling look like a pound, clothes off the peg look like models, and I had Helen's great good taste to copy.

Our long, light flat on the top floor of No. 82 was very pleasant. Blonde furniture, introduced by Syrie Maugham, was the thing, so I had stripped pine in the dining-room. I think this was a mistake, for Helen was polite about it, but there was never a similar piece in either of her gracious homes. The colouring was soft muted tones, so necessary for highly-strung people like me. My beautiful small Steinway grand piano had a short life there; I felt too shy to play when Edward was around, for he loved great music well enough to conduct it. All my furniture from Cadogan Gardens fitted in quite happily, to my surprise, for Cadogan Gardens was vast compared with Portland Place. Then we added my portrait.

Uncle Edgar had arranged to have me painted by Mary McEvoy, widow of Ambrose McEvoy, whom he had discovered and presented to the world. My portrait was considered the portrait of the year when it was hung in the Royal Academy, but I thought I looked like a frog! Mary McEvoy then painted a full-length one of Edward in his saffron kilt and green hill jacket against a misty Scottish background, with Heather close by his side. How well she caught his good looks and fey quality. I have both these portraits. I only hope that some day, when memories fade, his will find favour among his noble ancestors.

Bolts and chains became the order of the day on all doors at No. 82. I stupidly thought that they were to keep burglars out but I found that they were really there not to let the creditors in! I got into such a state of nerves whenever I heard the lift coming up or the door bell ring. And those mysterious notes so often found on the steering wheel of the car that Edward was quick to see and quicker to stuff in his pocket! What were they? When I asked he dodged the question.

All this attempt to protect me led to mistrust, and nothing is more damning to a marriage than that. The giving and receiving becomes guarded, and only a kind of loving remains. Much that I had heard that was detrimental to Edward I disregarded or refused to listen to, because I wanted to believe in

77

him and our life together more than anything else on earth. I still think that I was right.

Let's get away from it all and go north! Queenie Beckett, who had lent us her house in Yorkshire for the first part of our honeymoon, now offered us her little farm, which she called 'Farmie', on lease for a few months. It could have been out of *Wuthering Heights*, it was so like it, miles away from anywhere or anyone on the moors. This was lease number three, but the fishing was not good enough, Edward said, so we did not stay very long.

We went back to London for a bit, then to Scotland, where we took a little grey stone lodge on the Isle of Mull on a wonderful lonely loch. What a view! It was superb! I loved this place and so did the dogs; I tried to make it pretty and cosy, as I always did wherever I went, even with other people's unlovely things.

The lodge belonged to Lord Masserene and Ferrard, who lived at Knock Castle with his lovely wife Jean, who was seldom there. He let it to us for the summer to see if we would like to take it on a long lease. We stayed on until nearly the end of October, the month when the stags roar. I had never heard such a sound before. At first it startled me, then I started to listen for it and liked it; when the moon was high at night, the haunting sound would echo down the loch. We spent a lot of time on the loch in a boat, fishing—at least Edward fished while I watched. When we neared the top of the loch we used to pull in at the side and walk on the moor with the dogs. As this was the stags' mating season one had to be careful not to go too near. Never get between a stag and a hind! It was nearly my last walk in my wellingtons! High up on the hill a stag saw me, and a hind was near—too near. Up shot his antlered head and down the hill he tore after me! Edward shouted at me to grab Clover and get into a hole, crouch down, and be still. Well, you try to be still hanging on to a shouting spaniel with a roaring stag after you! He got within a hundred yards and lost the wind, while I lost ten pounds with fright! He moved off and so did we, as fast as we could run to the boat.

We were always alone like this, except for the dogs, out on

78

the loch or on the hills, always hand in hand and happy together. No one came to visit us and we saw few friends, except for a couple of evenings at Knock. We seemed safe so far away from London, but the trout were too big or too small and the creditors traced us, so that was the last we saw of Mull. Oh dear, would we never be able to settle and stay put?

Back again to Portland Place. Thank God we at least had this to ring the changes, and the D'Abernons to be with. There was always such a lot to do. Helen asked us often to her luncheons and dinners, where we met the distinguished and the great. I don't know which you would have called the Prime Minister, Ramsay MacDonald, and Augustus John; anyway they were often at St James' Place. Once, when I sat between these two gentlemen, and was being passed the sweet with strawberries on top, I scooped up all the berries, thinking they were three feet deep, to the merriment of Ramsay MacDonald. Helen was not at all amused, and when the Prime Minister saw this, he smiled at me and said, 'Aye, and bonnie they are.' I could have kissed him. Augustus John was so in his cups that he had missed the fun.

I never missed a chance to blot my copybook. Even so, I was invited everywhere and often asked to open fêtes and bazaars or give away prizes. This I dreaded, because I could never remember whether you gave the prize to the winner before or after you shook him or her by the hand. I still don't know! When I had to present a silver cup to the winning polo team at Stoke D'Abernon, I got so fussed that I gave the cup to the captain, but I shook hands with the entire team!

We went to Covent Garden quite often and shared our two seats for *The Ring* with Uncle Edgar, who tired easily because of his illness. We would go to the whole cycle and one of us would slip into his seat during the intermission. Edward taught me *The Ring* with all its motifs and I learned to love it as much as he did. Then too, Edward and Siegfried are rather alike; but poor Brunhilde, even she couldn't swing it.

During the lulls between storms, it was fun dressing Edward up, for he took little interest in his appearance and usually looked like a gamekeeper. Even so, he always looked who and what he was. But oh, how rewarding it was to choose well-cut suits for him that made him look 'every inch a duke' as they say. It made him proud of himself, and to be at his side made even me feel 'every inch a duchess'.

Then I was commanded by Their Majesties to attend a ball at the Palace—and all by myself!

So they had given me a torch to carry! What an honour, what a responsibility. No lady is ever bidden to a function at the Palace without her lord, master or duke, to enjoy his rank and privileges alone. This was recognition indeed—and explained the twinkle I saw in Queen Mary's eyes. How informed and observant the royal family is.

Helen told me that I should sit on the duchess' bench, which is on the right of the royal dais in the Throne Room. 'You are the Premier Duchess of Ireland,' she said, 'and will take precedence over the other duchesses, but as it will be your first appearance at Court don't sit on the front bench, which is your right, nor the top, nor the middle, but just behind and near the front.' I can't say that this was exactly clear or filled me with the confidence and assurance I sadly needed in my stage fright. Remember I had to go alone, knowing nothing, neither the form, the courtiers, the other duchesses, nor even where the bench was!

Helen placed her glorious diamond tiara, shaped like a crown, that sparkled like white heat, on 'my bonnie brown hair', as Edward called it; her wedding gift of emeralds and diamonds she pinned on my front. She stood behind me as we looked in the mirror together, and smiled. 'You will make us all proud,' she said.

The car was at the door; her Rolls with her chauffeur and footman on the box was mine for the evening. Trembling from head to foot in my wonderful dress, ermine wrap and borrowed jewels, I set off to the Palace like Cinderella. Well, I had wanted pomp and circumstance and here it was! Mother had always wanted me to shine, so shine I must, but could I? Why not? I had what it took, even if I was way out of my depth and an American. I had been asked, hadn't I, and with all Helen's diamonds, car and words of wisdom—none of which I could remember—how could I miss? Surely someone would smile upon me, please?

As the car drove up to the door and the footman leapt off the box to open it and hand me down, I froze with terror and nearly said, 'Let's go home!' But there was no turning back. I was already on the stairs and the car had gone. Up the red carpeted stairs I went to leave my wrap and try to find my way through all those tiaras, satin knee breeches, court dress and uniforms. Where, oh where was that wretched bench? Happily and finally, Gold Stick in Waiting, Sir Harry Stonor, saw me. I can't think how, as he was nearly blind, but thank God he did! Handsome in his full regalia, he bowed and said, 'How nice to see you, Duchess. May I take you to your place?' I nearly embraced him with relief and joy. There can't be many American girls who have seen what I saw that night, and been part of it. Certainly not alone. I knew that the young Duke of Grafton was to take me in to supper, as this information had been enclosed with my invitation, but supper seemed a long way off. All I wanted to do was to get to that bench, and sit there for ever.

'Make way, make way,' said Sir Harry, as he so carefully steered me through that tremendous and magnificent gathering, through miles and miles of red carpet and red velvet; through the general company who stand and look behind the long red silken rope; through members of the royal household and distinguished guests from all over the world, wearing their orders and heirlooms, and on and on to the royal dais at the far end of the room, and at last the duchess' bench!

There it was, just a small tier of red velvet benches upon which only duchesses could sit, except for the top row where the marchionesses sat. Many eyes were upon me and lorgnettes raised as I stood where Sir Harry had left me, trying to find the right place to sit. As it was my first time at Court, Helen had said, 'Just behind the front row.'

It looked rather full. Well, I'd try here on the second row, where there was a place. As I looked up to mount my bench,

I noticed a kindly smiling face watching me from above. It was the Duchess of Hamilton and Brandon. 'We are all rather old up here,' she said. 'We did not expect to see anyone as young and lovely as you. You are the youngest in the realm you know.'

Bless her, I thought, and I began to feel warm again and happy. I will never forget her welcome as long as I live.

What a sight I beheld! Hundreds of glittering guests softly murmuring below as they moved about. The little band all in red playing high up in the gallery at the far end opposite the royal dais. The ambassadresses were seated on their bench opposite to ours on the left of the royal dais, while the ambassadors chatted to them all waiting with grace and poise for the fanfare to announce the arrival of the King and Queen. What a sight! What a sight! Never had I or mother dreamed of anything like this! How could we; it only happened in books!

I was transfixed with the beauty of it all, and sat there holding my breath, for it was real! How I wished that 'My Imp' was there to take his place and see what he too had never seen, yet given me the right to enjoy. What an enormous room, and what a hard seat! Perhaps it was because I was sitting on the edge of it; yes, I was ... there, that was better, I thought, as I relaxed a little and got more used to being where I was.

Suddenly, the fanfare. The trumpets sounded, and Their Majesties were coming. We stood up in silence as Gold Stick in Waiting came walking backwards through the great doors opposite, followed by Her Majesty Queen Mary, on the arm of the Prince of Wales—the King was still ill—followed by the Duke and Duchess of York, Prince George, the Duke and Duchess of Gloucester, Princess Mary and other members of the royal family.

As they came slowly, we all swept low curtseys and the gentlemen bowed their heads. How could anyone so small wear so many jewels, orders and sashes and not even look tired! As they approached the royal dais, there was a roll of drums, then 'God Save the King'. Then we were allowed to sit. By this time, I had grown quite fond of my seat and thought it soft as down!

I watched what the other duchesses did, but they just sat

like me. Then I saw coming towards us Sir Harry and Queen Mary. Good Lord, I thought, what do I do now? All the duchesses rose and curtsied low as Her Majesty came up to me. 'We welcome you here and hope to welcome you both here very soon,' she said. God bless her, I thought, and wanted to kiss her. Yes, this we would do, come wind, come weather. Surely this would restore 'My Imp' to his senses, his allegiance and his place in the sun.

After Her Majesty had honoured me thus, all the other duchesses made me feel welcome among them. The Aga Khan came up and asked if he might sit beside me. What a jolly, smiling, friendly fellow, an immense man with immense charm. He had an eye for a pretty woman and seemed to know everyone there. He pointed out many well-known and distinguished people and made me feel that the world up there on my velvet plank was a better place than before he came. He was grandly dressed for the occasion, wearing medals and a sash, and enormous horn-rimmed spectacles which made his face look bigger than it was. I liked him. He seemed to know that I was strange and very much on my own, and went out of his way to be nice to me.

Sir Harry came and told me that the procession was about to form and that the Duke of Grafton would be taking me in to supper. But where was he? Oh where, oh where, was my duke? The procession was halted. As Premier Duchess of Ireland I had to go first after the royal family. No one could move as I had no escort! What a dilemma! Court officials, guests and flunkies searched for my missing duke, and found him hiding behind a curtain near the duchess' bench. Very frightened, very young, and very shy, I felt that we were both in a goldfish bowl swimming upstream.

At last we took our places in the waiting procession and moved through all the distinguished guests and the general company and on to the Gold Plate Room, where supper awaited us. Grafton clung to me more than I to him. 'I have never been to a Court function before,' he said, 'and I was afraid that you would be like the duchess in *Alice in Wonderland*, and not the young and beautiful lady that you are. I am sorry that I took fright.'

The Gold Plate Room is where the gold plate is kept on display in glass show-cases when it is not in use, as it was tonight. I had never eaten off gold before but I did not eat much; I was too excited. People whom I did not know came up and talked to me, including the Prince of Wales and several members of the royal household and courtiers. I was well looked after by my timid duke and the ever-watchful Gold Stick in Waiting. He seemed at all times to know where I was, even though he could hardly see and had the whole function to deal with. I dare say that he had promised Helen D'Abernon to look after me, for which I was truly grateful.

Then we were to process back to the Throne Room to resume our places. My little duke and I were on our own now at the head of our fellow peers and peeresses, and very happy indeed, when suddenly a peeress, wife of a former Ambassador to Rome who was not in the procession, beckoned to me from the side to come over to her. I couldn't make out what she was trying to tell me, so alas, I stepped out of the procession to see what she wanted.

She took me by the arm and said, 'It's all over now. Come and have a proper supper with Ron and me.' Nobody had told me about the strict Court protocol of such an occasion, so the procession went on without me, back to the duchess' bench . . . and everyone noticed my absence . . . even the Queen. Had I been taken ill? What could have happened, for surely I must know that no one could leave the procession or go away before Her Majesty?

Lady R. may have been hungry, but she had failed to observe that 'it' was *not* all over . . . but it was all over for me. The torch I had been given to carry which had made me so proud, went out like a flame . . . and not long after that wrecked evening the Duke of Grafton's life went out too. He was killed winning a car race in Ireland.

Would I ever be asked again or be able to fulfil the promise I made to myself when the queen of all queens offered her hand of welcome to us both? No, not my Edward, alas! He just couldn't stay the course. But I was asked again and again, and still am now, just as I started and have always gone . . . completely on my own.

Chapter 7

As I write and reflect on the richness and grandeur of the world I have moved in, touched, but never possessed or really become a part of, I wonder how really hollow was my crown, my entrée, my victory and my defeat. How could any man born, like Edward, to everything make such a disaster of it? Elusive, gentle, generous, lovable, kind, and so well bred and good to look at—why? Being a gentle mender at heart and preferring to make something out of nothing, rather than nothing out of something, I went on and on believing in Santa Claus.

Edward was safer in the country, where he was happiest and free. Here he was home, and being together with our dogs and music we found a sweet relationship that made up for rough times. So on and on we went, searching for the perfect place where the trout were right and the price was right. And I signed seventeen leases in three years!

Miles and miles we drove with numerous orders-to-view, looking for the home I had dreamed of ever since I could dream. We raced through the countryside of England, Scotland and Wales, no longer in the Bentley—that had gone the way of other expensive toys—but in a Ford station wagon sent from USA by my mother. Of course it couldn't reach 113 miles an hour, our usual cruising speed, but it had to beat any rabbit none the less and always did!

There is nothing I deplore more than waste: waste of time, life, looks, money and opportunity. Perhaps this drove me on and gave me the purpose I needed. We left Scotland alone for a while, and looked at places in England and Wales: one, so promising on paper, in Derbyshire, where I found Stevenson, our first chauffeur who became my devoted servant, a protector, whom I trusted. He was a handsome young yokel, an

86

excellent driver, with that flair for style that always pleased me. We did not take the house, but the chauffeur came to us as soon as it was sold. Teaching him his way about London, where he had never been, took some time, as did trying to understand his accent: 'You can get abaat if you know the coooots,' he would say, and for the life of me I hadn't a clue what he meant!

We then went to Somerset and took a charming place, Colinshayes Manor, with the option to buy or take on a long lease. Lease number five, and the usual dreary business of cleaning, polishing, rearranging other people's things to try to make it look and feel like home. We brought our own staff, including a smartly turned-out chauffeur in family livery, buttons and crown in his cap, our cook, Mrs Wood, and Sayeres the butler, recommended by the Becketts, who used to sniff so much that I had to tell him to stop.

It's up to the man of the house to deal with the men servants or they get out of hand, but Edward, being shy, seldom showed or used any authority. The servants seemed to like him well enough, and of course he was a duke, which upped their station in life, but being the cunning breed that they are, they took every advantage, especially of the green American. I always had my maid with me, and we also took Kathleen, the house-parlourmaid.

After a few months in the Frome Valley, long enough for Clover to get stung on her nose by a wasp and for my mother and Jimmy to pay us a very short visit, I could see the signs of Edward's restlessness, so once again we folded our tents and stole away.

We kept our base in Portland Place, where Edward's small dressing-room was an untidy mess of racing books, unpaid bills, threatening letters—and trouble. Here he used to ask one or two of his friends and more than a few hangers-on. I tried to put up with bad news, which was easier to take than the con men and con women, who were really the dregs! Edward seemed as at ease in the pantry as with his own kind. Bookies, hooligans and money lenders flattered him, as did their women.

But to the gentry, he was a charming person, who had let down the side, *their* side.

There was another life, too, in London, full of music, interest and invitations to balls, dinners and functions, that never ceased to delight the girl from USA. There were also the faithful attentive D'Abernons and the wonderful family place they had bought at Stoke D'Abernon on the river Mole. It was well named, for it crept along. Helen's taste and touch were magic and the house, garden and chapel, famous for its brasses, sprang into beauty. There was the great hall with black and white marble floor, the drawing-room hung in blue silk damask—and the pictures! There was a full-length portrait of Helen by Sargent, and one of Uncle Edgar by Augustus John; then Gainsboroughs, Turners, curtains, flowers and exquisite furniture from her palazzo in Rome. It was a privilege to stay there, as we did several times, and I did—on my own as usual—for more week-ends and weeks than I can count. I loved these two, Helen and Uncle Edgar, and felt their genuine concern, affection and wish to help rebuild our house of cards.

I used to meet Margot Asquith there. Her sharp hatchet-like face and voice of authority sprang from a brilliant brain and the kindest heart. I used to walk with her and Ramsay MacDonald and just listen to them: something I would always rather do than talk. Not that I could have bowled them over even if I had tried. Still, I prefer to listen.

I had such a lot of things I heard and saw to think about and store up like a squirrel to feed off for months and months. The Gladwyns, then Jebb, were also great friends of the D'Abernons, and I met them often at Stoke. Cynthia Jebb, now Lady Gladwyn, was and is like an exquisite Dresden figure with her fair colouring and prematurely white hair. To these famous and important people, including Augustus John and many others, I was the niece of the house, nothing more, nothing less. I contributed little, except, as Helen put it, 'a pleasing countenance and willing ear'. So they accepted me and I was well content.

All my life I have longed for a home of my own, so I was

always ready to try again. There were three more places that we took, but not for long. Edward found one in Hampshire at Alresford, right on a gentle river that flowed through the garden. It was fresh and clear and I could see and count the trout. Surely this would delight my restless one? The fresh green, well-mown stretch of lawn between the river and the house pleased me so much that I wanted to roll on it, and the house was lovely. We negotiated, and the lease was drawn up, but a judgment summons was also drawn up and the owner withdrew.

Then another owner in Wales, after doing a little research, came up with an even more definite excuse. That was the ninth lease put before me to sign. Better try Ireland again, or near 'the Priest'. What about that sweet place Sudeley House, up that long lane to nowhere: newly done up, empty of everything, just waiting to be moved into? Fresh, clean, with central heating and two bathrooms! Luxury indeed, in highly civilized, highly uncomfortable England. How I wanted that mellow stone house surrounded by lavender, where all you could hear were the bees. If I had had my way, I would have moved in that day, but when I saw Edward's face, which said, 'What no fish; just bees!' that was that.

What about that long, low Cotswold house on the hill at Stow-on-the-Wold? I had always had my eye on that, but it had not been to let. Maybe now? Yes, by jove, it was. Lease number ten coming up, and jolly nice too, so I grabbed it and down we went with our load of servants, dogs, household needs and clothes in time for Christmas. Here we had our first big tree and trimmed it on the night before Christmas, when all was still. It even snowed, proper snow that one seldom sees in southern England. Enough for Edward and me to slide down the hills on trays as I used to do as a child in New Canaan. The frost and snow gave a tang to the air. It felt like home and was fun.

Then I got a pain in the middle of my stomach, right in the middle of the night! It was quite a to-do, with mother on the telephone fearing the worst, and no local doctor to rouse from his slumber. At cock crow I was rushed to London with Edward driving at his usual pace, to be X-rayed. My poor appendix was kicking up a row and had to come out at once. Before you could say knife, I got it deep and swift.

Sir Crisp-English, produced by Dr Fraser Carey, who said he was known as 'the appendix king', was the surgeon, and whipped it out in the small private nursing home at 17 Park Lane with such skill that I can hardly find the scar to this day. How tender and loving 'My Imp' was to me. The night before the operation, surely the worst night in anyone's life, Edward came and brought me a wee black woolly lamb. 'I can't be with you when they put you to sleep in the morning,' he said, 'so hold fast to this little black sheep, because I am the black sheep.' How long I held it I don't know, but I had it when I drifted away, and I had it when I floated back to consciousness, and my very dear husband who was just where I had left him hours ago, smiling with relief and happiness. To this day, like the tiny scar, I still have the little black lamb.

While I was in the nursing home recovering from the operation, King George died, and the great slow solemn procession passed our windows. It trailed up Hyde Park on its mournful way to Westminster Abbey where the well-loved monarch was to lie in state. Behind the gun carriage, where the coffin lay draped with the Union Jack with the crown, orb and sceptre on top, walked the Prince of Wales, now the king, his brothers, the Duke of York, the Duke of Gloucester and the Duke of Kent. Behind them in a closed carriage sat Queen Mary, heavily veiled, with Princess Mary by her side. Was it weakness, or sadness, or the dragging tread to Guards' bands playing Chopin's 'Funeral March' that filled my eyes with tears and my heart with sorrow? Sorrow, I think, for that wonderful, lonely queen who had smiled upon me.

Somewhere, we had met a colonel and his unobtrusive wife, who owned Isercleran, or St Clerens in Galway. We saw them again; they persuaded us to go over and have a look at their place and see if we would like to take it for a few months with the option of a long lease. So it was now back again to Eire, where we stayed at inns and looked at Isercleran and other places in Connemara. It was a pretty Georgian house in an immense park with a small river and to my delight a ha-ha. We took it and sent for our possessions.

The ha-ha, according to our little pack of spaniels, separated the natural from the supernatural. I have stayed at several places where ghosts walked and things went bump in the night, such as Kinnaird, where I heard the heavy tread as the clock struck twelve, and Crathes, Guthrie and Carton. But I had reservations. Had I really heard a ghost? I had married an earth-bound spirit, but he never walked at night: on the contrary he slept like a stone when our world was spinning like a top.

I never really believed in haunted places till our dogs proved it to be so. Walking with the dogs was a happiness I sadly missed in my city life. Every day we would walk along by the river to the ha-ha, where all five spaniels would go no further. There they would stop and stiffen, their tails up, their hair up, their ears up, and they would growl and bark as if the banshee were after them. Maybe it was, for they would run yelping in all directions, away from whatever it was they saw. I thought this was nonsense, and that it must be a deer or fox, and lifted each spaniel down the other side of the ha-ha, but not a hope—they were away like streaked lightning and into the river. All, that is, except Shammy Shouter, as I called Shamrock, who shouted such a lot: she, poor frightened little thing, had a fit. I picked her up and stuck her head inside my jacket where it was dark; the terrible trembling, jerking and foaming at the mouth passed, leaving the limpest, weakest, semi-demi-spaniel for me to carry the rest of the way.

There was a pile of rocks under a thorn tree, where the little people are supposed to live and a small wood that the dogs would never go near. Even if you carried them into it, as I did, you would wish you hadn't. They saw something, of that I am convinced, and their fear was real and consistent. It happened at the same places every day that we were at Isercleran, but happily, never in the house. So this spacious manor house was not haunted, or the dogs would have told us so.

I rearranged the house, and please God this would be for keeps! It had style. It had lodge gates, and I had always wanted lodge gates. They belonged to the privileged classes, they made you feel important and mistress of your acres, or so it seemed to this young American girl so impressed by the splendours of Britain that were only borrowed.

I did wonders to the walled garden, which was as neglected as the house. I got rid of countless flower beds which one tripped over wherever one went and made the lawns flow like green velvet down to the river. Another Brooklyn dream, for it was there that I had seen my first big lawn and it gave me the kind of pleasure that I have never ceased to delight in. Here it was, and I'd make the most of it. For the first time since our marriage I knew peace.

We would walk, fish, make plans for doing up the house and making Ireland our home, as I had always thought we should do. For wasn't Ireland where Edward, Premier Duke of Ireland, belonged? Yes, we would take it on a very long lease, as it could not be bought, being the family home of the Coles. I would keep that big four-poster bed in my vast bedroom, where a bat would fly in, fan my nose with its tiny whirring wings and squeak at me. Edward caught it in a fishing net and threw it out of the window, where it tried to bite off its legs to free itself! When I saw what was happening, I ran for the chauffeur who saved it just in time!

Our only neighbours were the Bowes-Dalys. He was master of foxhounds and their place marched with Isercleran. We were asked there to lunch; I liked Diana Daly as soon as we met and hoped that she would become a friend. I felt a little shy with Colonel Bowes-Daly, but not at all with his wife. I hoped that she needed a friend too. She was the sister of the Duchess of Buccleuch, who is considered a beauty, and who now lives next to me here in Grosvenor Square. She is the only duchess out of the four of us in the building who rejoices in a duke! We have met only six times in twenty-one years: once over the dustbins and five times running down the hall. She is good to look at, but I found even more warm beauty in her sister's face.

We stayed over a year at Isercleran—a long time for us—and to this day I believe that if there ever was any chance at all for our marriage to sustain its tough passage and the rather restless spirit of 'My Imp', it was at Isercleran. This timeless, dateless land has an easy charm that takes you over; if you can't lie down in the hay there and let the world go by, you never will.

But the inevitable telegram came—not so easy to hide in Ireland where the delivery of one was the event of the day. It meant trouble. Off went Edward to London where he stayed for several weeks: God knows where, or with whom and why. I waited and waited with the dogs, until finally he came back and we settled down again to a temporary lull before the next storm. Then he suddenly said that he must go to London again! This time we all packed up and returned to 82 Portland Place. I think there was a jinx on it from the start, or on me, for the strangest things happened there.

On Thanksgiving Day, mother and Jimmy, my stepfather, came to lunch with us. The pleasant occasion had an unpleasant sequel. It was on that day that my engagement ring, my ruby bracelet and the carefully chosen and designed charm bracelet that Edward had given me disappeared. I had left them in a tiny blue dish on my dressing table in our bedroom at the far end of the long hall. The window near the fire escape was open a crack. The police were called and came at once; the newspapers made much of 'Duchess Robbed'.

Another day, I was rung up by an unknown solicitor, while Edward was on one of his marathon jaunts in the car to Scotland with Heather by his side, to tell me that May Ethridge had been found dead with her head in a gas oven and would I bury her! She, poor little unhappy soul, had been Edward's first wife and mother of Gerald. She was kept very much in the background, and they had compelled her to call herself May Murray and she was not allowed to use any of the family names. She had been a beautiful chorus girl when Edward married her, much against the will of his family and the trustees. But Edward was like that; to tell him not to do a thing was to make him do it.

I had the greatest difficulty in getting Edward to go to her funeral. Gerald would not go at all. They were an unusual pair, these two, to say the least! Soon after the funeral, with the publicity it was bound to bring and photographs of Edward paying his final respects to one who had taken her own life, there was an urgent need to leave the country and quick! So back to the big sparkling city where we had met nearly two years before on the day that my beloved Gyp wanted to see pancakes flipped in the air.

Me, in my pretty grey feather hat that Edward had shot for me—I found the pellet in the graceful heron who used to stand and fish on one leg in the little river outside my window at Isercleran. And Edward, suddenly a boy again, and dressed at long last like a duke. How little he cared for his appearance and yet how nice he could look. He felt happy and safe at sea, anyway until we reached New York, where the cameras flashed and reporters came in dozens and, except for one picture of us together, Edward dodged them.

We went first to Mayfair House, where mother and Jimmy lived, and where they had got a room for us. Not for long, as Edward seemed uneasy and restless as always, so we decided to have a second honeymoon in Jamaica. Surely that would be far enough away from whatever it was that was chasing him.

What a beautiful place it is, with its hills, sea, brilliant birds, singing people, and egrets sitting in hundreds in the trees. It was the singing that I never forgot, the singing of the Negroes as they cut the sugar cane at sunrise and as the moon sets. They sang in rhythm as they swung their knives, and the grief and happiness rang out from the hills until you too were caught up in it and wanted to sing and swing with them.

The enormous flying cockroaches upset me, however. They would zoom in at night like rockets and knock you for six if their aim was good. By day they ate your clothes, so we came down from the hills and went as paying guests to a plantation a few miles from Montego Bay to stay with a Mr and Mrs

Robinson. This I loved. No cockroaches or horrors here, just blackbirds that came in dozens to join us at breakfast on the terrace at six o'clock in the morning. They sat on the table, even on our heads! That was the cool of the day, when the parrots flashed through the trees and the world was awake.

Later we would go down to the lagoon to swim where the water was so clear that we could see the bottom. Too clear, for I dived deep and there it was right smack in front of me, glaring at me from its niche—a parrot fish. What a face! He didn't like mine either and spat at me as he shot out of his hole; I just beat him to the top! After that I looked carefully through a glass before diving deep to see if that brilliantly coloured angry face were around, but I never saw the parrot fish again. The only other strange face I saw was on land, when I looked down and saw a praying mantis with enormous eyes praying on my instep. He didn't pray long, I can tell you, for creepy crawlies are not my favourite pets.

We stayed nearly a month in Jamaica, which I for one thoroughly enjoyed; but I don't think it was exactly Edward's cup of tea. There was nothing for him to shoot, fish or chase, except mosquitoes, and that was not his idea of fun. So we went back, first to New York, then London, where he who fights and runs away must fight again another day.

Once back in London I didn't give in in spite of our hopeless position, but called it a challenge and went out and got myself a smashing long black velvet off-the-shoulder ermine-trimmed evening dress, which, to my happy surprise, I wore to the Palace when Their Majesties' Lord Chamberlain commanded my presence again: alone, as before. This time, I promise you I knew my way, and when I got to the duchess' bench I sat down with a bang right in the middle of the front row in all my ducal splendour.

Edward, Prince of Wales, King of England, had given up his throne 'for the woman I love', Mrs Wallis Simpson. Much of the world was stunned and all of England wept. Their Prince Charming had let them down. It was a deep personal wound to the butcher, the baker, the candlestick-maker, and to all the peers and people of the realm. One listened to that moving broadcast of a king taking leave of his country and his people, and by choice, with every sort of emotion, as I was to listen to an even graver broadcast not too far hence when the Prime Minister told us: 'We are at war!' Somehow, nearly three years before that day when our lives stood still, it was in the air that night at the Palace. Two nights before the ball there was the fatal crash of the Hesse plane on its way to England. Their Majesties, formerly the Duke and Duchess of York, were giving the ball for the King of the Belgians. It was too late to cancel the evening, so we were told to wear mourning. It was indeed the prelude.

Strange that the Prime Minister, Neville Chamberlain, came to sit with me on our bench, as he had the right to do. Isercleran had been his home, too, for his wife was a Cole, so we had much to talk about. He told me about De Valera, who had played a small part in my life at the time of the recent coronation. We had been bidden to attend, so our splendid robes belonging to Edward's family were got ready for us. Not long before the great ceremony was to take place, we were informed that we could not go to the Abbey. Edward, being an undischarged bankrupt, would not be allowed to attend. What a shaming blow! However, De Valera stepped in and asked if I could go along to represent Eire. But Eire was not allowed to be represented, as she was not part of the Empire any more, so we, Edward and I, sat it out at Stoke D'Abernon and watched Helen go forth looking like a goddess to attend as ex-ambassadress to Germany—the occasion of a lifetime.

De Valera was at that time trying to make a deal with Neville Chamberlain and the Prime Minister told me that evening how elusive he was. He came over from Eire to Downing Street to come to terms with England. He left his hat, then went in to be received by Mr Chamberlain. No sooner had he sat down than he got up, said: 'Where's my hat?' and left!

Handsome, oh yes, to the pleasure of all who beheld him, was the young, tall, elegant King Leopold of the Belgians that night, as he led the royal procession with our Queen. His lovely Queen Astrid, lay in a cemetery on the hill where she had met

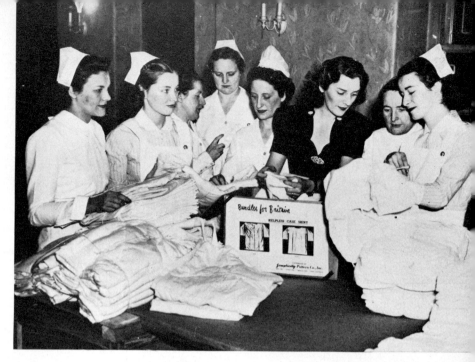

Sorting donations for British hospitals

Four prisoners of war presenting a bouquet to their overseas Chairman

Carton, the seat of the Duke of Leinster

The Italian music room at Carton

Feeding the pigeons in Venice

The occasion of my first presentation at Court. I was wearing a Norman Hartnell dress

With Cecil Beaton who designed the Queen of Spades costume I am wearing

Our tall studio drawing
room at 101 Cadogan
Gardens

My first marriage – Clare
Van Neck and his
American bride

Arriving in New York after my
marriage to the Duke of Leinster

Edward with Clover and Heather

Presenting trophies to the winning Polo team at Stoke D'Abernon

My father

My mother

Myself, aged two

Mother and me in our Brooklyn garden

Princess Maud, the Earl of Southesk and the local vicar at a fair near Aberdeen

her death when he, the King, was driving too fast and struck a tree. You could still see the shock and sorrow in his face, as he sat there on the dais at the right of the Queen, watching the magnificent sight with detachment.

There were signs of mourning everywhere, especially on the royal dais, the ambassadress' bench and the duchess' bench. I remember how well mauve became the Duchess of Kent, and silver the Queen. The dreadful air crash had killed an entire royal party, including the Princess of Hesse's child, who was born between the sky and the earth as the plane hit the world below. The shock of this hideous tragedy was very much with us and toned down the evening considerably.

However, the Queen opened the ball with King Leopold, and the distinguished guests and general company moved on to the floor in couples. This time my escort was the exciting, good-looking Duke of Rutland, who took me to twirl a measure and later to supper. This time my duke did not get lost, and I walked in the procession on his arm with proud pleasure, nor did I leave his side as we processed back to the bench.

There were two incidents that night at the Palace that I won't forget. One was the moment in the Gold Plate Room when I heard a sinister voice say: 'Duchess, may I get you some salmon, . . . here, do take mine.' I turned, and looked first at the cold eyes of the speaker, the German Ambassador, then at the cold fish on a cold gold plate; I looked at von Ribbentrop, and said: 'No thank you,' and promptly accepted exactly the same thing from the Duke of Kent. How rude can you get, or did I hear the wail of sirens of 1939?

The other event took place soon after I had returned to the duchess' bench. It was bold and thrilling, and caused everyone to hold their breath. A lovely peeress walked out to the centre of the empty state ballroom and just stood there completely alone facing the King of the Belgians. How beautiful she was in her shimmering dress, jewels and youth. No one missed this daring performance, least of all King Leopold for whom it was intended. I saw it happen, and was entranced. Gold Stick in Waiting must have given the signal for the band to play.

Quickly Her Majesty rose, and she and King George began to dance together. I too was being asked to dance, and made a beautiful curtsey, I hope, to a royal prince; like all British men, he had no more idea how to lose himself in the music and let himself go than the next man. Dancing was my happiness under the Stars and Stripes, but under the Union Jack, you can keep it. I was even called the 'Waltzing Duchess', but try to find a partner who knew a waltz from musical chairs! The English milord may bowl you over by the way he wears his clothes, the way he walks and talks, but on the dance floor give me the American who doesn't know how to wear his clothes or walk or talk, every time.

In spite of the lamentable fact that even His Royal Highness could not tell which feet were his, I was swept up in his fairyland. The 'boy meets girl' touch had added romance to this scene of splendour; I was part of it, and my heart sang with the joy of it. Yet, deep down somewhere within myself, I felt that it would never be like this again: not only for me, but for each and all of us. How right I was.

I was happy with my conquests—a prime minister, a noble duke, a royal prince, and Hitler's spy—until my world was threatened too.

Chapter 8

How could you have the flight of the heron, the cry of the curlew, the leap of the trout and yellow primroses all at the same time and all in the same place, and, on a song? You just couldn't, and eat.

The answer was to burn our boats and compromise. Give up our long, light flat in Portland Place, take an unfurnished house in the country and call it a day. Better try Gloucestershire again near 'the Priest'. He was Edward's only loyal friend, even though he was old enough to be his father, but there was true affection between them; perhaps because they were both lovable rogues, in their way. I also wanted to lose the awful con men who were under my feet.

We found a likely place, or rather 'the Priest' did. It was Waterlane House, tucked away where only the larks rose and fell. It was built of lovely warm Cotswold stone, just the right size, empty and waiting. I took it on a long lease after having it surveyed and generally vetted locally. We stayed with 'the Priest' and Marion while I did it up from top to bottom to my heart's delight. How long had I waited to do just this! Even before it was completely finished we decided to move the furniture in and camp. But we never even camped. The well, our only water supply, was contaminated! Waterlane was not on the mains for electricity or water, so this meant that a new well would have to be dug. A dead loss, and the straw that almost broke this camel's back. We all sat down and cried, none louder than the poor little 'Priest'.

Having lost our flat in the shuffle, we had to go somewhere, so I went to the Dorchester Hotel, while Edward went to Galway to have another look at the small white lodge on the island at Renvyle that we had seen together when we were at

99

Isercleran. It belonged to Oliver St John Gogarty, wit, poet
and writer of Ireland, whom we had met in Connemara, where
he used to walk the muddy lanes between the hedges of wild
fuschia, in a black city-slicker suit and evening slippers with
bows on them.

Gogarty offered us the lodge on lease. It was very remote,
and could be reached only by a boat which leaked faster than
you could row. You had to bail out like mad every crossing, or
sink. There was no electricity and no stairs. They had been forgotten, and a rickety affair was put up on the outside of the
house as an afterthought. When you wanted to go up to bed
and it rained—which was always—you put up an umbrella,
carried a torch and hoped for the best!

The lodge was the only house on the island; it was tiny and
bang in the middle of a fresh-water loch. All you could see were
the tall blue mountains, the Twelve Pins, and all you could
hear were the wild swans and the beat of their great wings like
thunder, as they flew two by two to join hundreds and hundreds
of others in Galway Bay, where they bobbed about, nested and
added to their numbers during the winter months.

We didn't take the island then, for it was too wild and too
far away even for Edward, and very hard to get to. So back he
came to London, and I could feel the same old longing for
Scotland. That was the one place he preferred every time, and
I too felt happy there. I loved the Scots, their hills, their tartan,
and the pibroch. They didn't rush you and gush you to see
what you were worth to them. They either liked you or they
didn't, and that was it.

We saw a picture in *Town and Country* of Inverawe House.
It was in Argyllshire, and from what one could read it seemed
to have everything we had dreamed of; all for only £400 a year,
and on a long lease unfurnished. There it was, far, far away
from trouble and the madding crowd of creditors, high up on
the bank of a lively river, full of trout—I hoped—with miles of
moor at the back where the red deer roamed and little tarns
sparkled in the sunlight. What a setting, what a find!

Edward saw it, sent for me and I fell in love with it on sight.

Literally on sight, when I saw in the distance the red ivy that covered the front of the house like a flame. It reminded me of autumn at home, where the reds and yellows of the trees and creepers blind you with their brilliance and beauty. I couldn't believe that such a perfect and grand place as this could ever become ours. It even had the lodge-gate-house I coveted. What I could do with this friendly, strong, well-built house! I could hardly wait. Surely this was our reward and the end of the rainbow at last. The dogs and Edward would have all the rabbits and trout they could chase for the rest of their lives.

We took it and, as usual, the lease for seven, fourteen, twenty-one years, was sent to me to sign. As I have explained before, Edward's signature was unacceptable, as he was an undischarged bankrupt. I wonder if it could have turned out worse if he had put his mark above the red seal? Then south to the Dorchester to arrange for the big haul to the place that was too good to be true. After so many false starts, this lease seemed a tremendous commitment; it startled me.

Being Sagittarius and possessing a sixth sense, a strange far-away bell was tolling. Was it a warning or was it nerves? Whatever it was, I held off for a couple of weeks; I couldn't really tell why. Edward was buzzing around as usual, doing I never knew what with I never knew whom, and always pacing the floor with a face of woe. Well, I should be used to that by now. Suddenly he would break into a smile when he saw my concern, and my spirits would lift. Even so, I went on stalling, even though I had now signed the lease. Finally, the owner of Inverawe got the wind up and said that if he did not receive the signed lease at once he would withdraw. What to do, what to do?

I had already chosen the carpets and curtains, collected a staff of servants, and told Harrods to have the furniture packed in vans ready for the long drive north. Yet I felt panic. Why? What was the matter with me? I must tell Edward about my misgivings and find out how it really was with him. We were lunching together that day, and going later to Memo White-foord for tea. I would ask him if it were safe, really safe for me to tell our solicitor to send off the lease. His preoccupation worried me. I told him while we lunched that I was still holding up the lease as it was such a big and final step to take, and I had to be sure that all was well before I let it go. He just laughed at me and said: 'Of course, darling, let it go. Send it off by all means.'

I let it go!

Immediately after lunch I went round to the solicitor and told him to post the lease. After that I went back to the hotel to have a big think and a little rest before Edward came to collect me and take me to tea in Hay Hill. There was a knock on the door; thinking it was Edward, I hurried to open it and found instead a very small freckled-faced page boy holding a silver salver on which lay a letter addressed to me in Edward's handwriting. But why, he would be here in a minute?

As I held the letter and closed the door, I felt rather strange and wanted to sit down, for somewhere in my head that bell was tolling louder and louder; or was it my heart beating? Yes, that must be it. I must pull myself together and read the letter, which was probably to tell me to meet him at Memo's. I was sitting on the bed as I opened the letter, which was two pages long. He had taken the dogs and the station wagon—and gone!

How long I had been lying on the floor I don't know. All I did know was that I was nearly under the bed that I had been sitting on, that I felt as weak as a kitten and that it was nearly dark. As I revived, I let out a shout: 'My God, the lease, I must stop the lease!' Shaking like a tree in the wind, I rang our solicitor.

Of course he had 'stepped out'. Why do doctors, dentists, bank managers and solicitors always 'step out' when you need them in a rush? I had to stop that lease, and fast. As I waited for him to ring back I read the terrible letter again, telling me that Edward was on his way to Renvyle as there was big trouble. He said that I had put up with too much and that he would give me a divorce if I wanted it, even though he loved me more than anyone or anything on earth.

I was weeping when the telephone rang and, to my relief, it

was the solicitor. I told him the dreadful story and about the bombshell of a letter. Had he posted the lease? Yes, he had, only a few minutes earlier in the post-box outside the Langham Hotel. Could it be got out? Well, that really was asking too much! Well, could he? You have to dynamite the British to make them jump to it. I said: 'Ring the Postmaster General and get permission to get the lease out of the box, if it is still there, and tell him why.'

Our solicitor did a double somersault, but he rang the Postmaster General, told the story and got permission; it was still there, and soon back in his hands. My guardian angel was so near I could almost touch his wings. St Raffael stood by my side, I was safe and the bell in my head rang no more.

Good-bye to the home that was too good to be true; and good-bye to my husband, who had spent all of his life running out on himself. Now he had run out on me.

What to do when you are married to a runner-outer and are left alone to face the music with no one to turn to? Only an hour before his letter came he had told me to be happy and send off the lease, knowing, as he must have done, that he was going to run for it. How do you feel or think or act when you have been hit with a wallop as hard as that? Do you run also? After all, I had no regular income of my own, and would be sued by the owner of Inverawe. I had no roots, no real friends, for they had drifted away when I married my black sheep. I had no family, and no need or reasons to stay. The only thing to do was to ring down the curtain and go home. But did I? No, poor fool me. I stayed right where I was. All by myself, with a view of St Paul's. Well not quite by myself for I had a tiny companion . . . a mini mini mouse who loved fudge. His getting the fudge the size of himself from off my bedside table intrigued me and I thought if he can manage his load . . . I can manage mine.

I was young, I had looks—or so the British had told me—and I had health and resilience, so I'd get to work on the whole lot of them, and win. Good fighting talk, but could I do it? I certainly had nothing more to lose, so I'd have a try. I wrote to

103

Edward, told him to stay where he was, and sent him ten
pounds a week to live on, there in that small white lodge on the
island of Renvyle.

I then got the list of his creditors and went to see each of
them, asking them to withdraw their petitions. Rogues, con
men, moneylenders and bookies, tradespeople and the like
couldn't have been more understanding, kind and helpful than
they were to me. I'll never forget this experience, which took
me many months. These visits to holes in the corner, the cold
tricky glances and, to my surprise, the trust and goodwill with
which I came away every time.

I told them how it really was; that I was the poorest American who ever wore a coronet, and that I still believed that if they
would give us another chance they would be reimbursed.
Mallaby-Deeley wanted us to buy back the life interest, and if
enough money could be raised from securities from the Leinster
estate, we would all live happily ever after. While I was at it,
I had several interviews with Sir Harry, whom I found charming and distinguished. Things were looking up, I thought, and
had every reason to think so. Almost all the creditors withdrew
their petitions. Mallaby-Deeley was with me, or so I thought,
and even the owner of Inverawe let me off the hook. I was
riding high, wide and handsome and, as they say, 'kept myself
to myself', for I didn't want anyone to know what had happened.

The only people who knew were 'the Priest' and Michael St
Aldwyn, who gave me the courage I needed so badly. He used
to take me dancing, and told me at great length how much he
admired me and my loyalty to my husband. He strengthened
my resolve and I loved him for it, for I had no one to talk to
but this faithful friend. Later on he married Diana, a wonderful
girl, became a minister in the government, and now has three
sons. After all these years I am proud to say he is still my friend.

One evening I sat next to Lord Darnley at a supper at a ball;
he asked me to lunch with him the following Sunday at his house
in the country and see his garden. How the British love to show
you their gardens, even if they are only a radish patch! I was

delighted. He was handsome and charming and it would open a whole new vista for me. Why I thought that he would be alone I don't know, but I was only one of several guests. He showed me round the house and many of his pastels, which were as delicate and fey as he was enormous and manly. In every picture there was the ghostlike figure of a woman; sometimes just a face faintly appearing in the background or lost in a tree, but it was always there. I asked him about it and he said: 'Yes, she is always there, but no one but you has noticed her.' We were then joined by others, and to this day I never found out who the lady in the tree was. But I did find out who the lady in his life was; she became the woman in mine.

Her name was Jo Wessel, a former Gaiety Girl, who was first married to Lord Churston, who died. By him she had had many children; the ex-Princess Aly Khan, Lady Ebury, Lady Cadogan, Lord Churston, and the former Duchess of Bedford. She had been born Jessie Smither, a daughter of a Sussex family who owned a bicycle shop, I was told. Her stage name had been Denise Orme. She was small, very pretty, with a lovely shaped face and great grey eyes under thick false eyelashes, which she used with skill to get what she wanted, anyway for a start.

She was then married to Tito Wessel, a Dane. They had one son. I should know, because they sat in front of Gyppy and me at a cinema in a hotel at Mürren when I was Mrs Van Neck, and she was the size of a house. She remembered me, and, of course I fell for her friendliness like a ton of bricks. How blind can a lonely heart get?

She seemed very much at home there with Cliff, as she called Darnley; we walked together and talked a lot after lunch, when the inevitable tour of the garden took place. Hungry for a cosy woman to talk to, she got more out of me than I realized, and before the garden walk was over she had asked me to lunch the following day at her house in St John's Wood and I had accepted. She was a clever huntress and was already sharpening her arrows, had I the sense to recognize it.

Jo gave me a delicious lunch in her enchanting house, which

she told me was one of several that she had bought, done up and sold at great profit. Her younger son was there at lunch, and also her pretty daughter, Denise, who was soon to be married. After lunch she really went to work on me. Jo told me how sorry she was for me and said that I was wasted on the bankrupt duke whom I had married. I should give the whole thing up and marry a young lord whom she had asked to dine the following evening, and would I come? Heavens, how did she know these things and not a minute lost?

How she broke me down! She knew how alone and vulnerable I was, and moved right into my plight, calculating every move and taking me in left, right and centre. Instead of being warned by it, I was warmed by it and jumped right in up to my small trusting brain. I wrote to 'My Imp' and told him about Jo, but he wrote back to tell me to run for my life, that she was not for me and a very dangerous woman! Fancy him seeing through anyone! I thought it was just the Connemara air, and went in deeper and deeper. Knowing how much I longed for a home and the joy of finding things for it, she introduced me to the Caledonian Market, where she, one of her adoring friends and I would go. I watched her bargain and buy things and was enthralled. If only I had a home and could do the same.

Jo sensed all this, and played on it much of the time, for didn't she have the very thing for me in Sussex? Beech Hill Farm, that she had bought and done up, as she had so many other places, and then sold at a profit. This would be perfect, and if I liked it and was determined to keep on with the folly of bailing out a worthless duke, she would consider letting it to us on lease. Clever, scheming Jo, she knew her stuff all right. So she moved right in and took over. I kept on writing to Edward saying how wonderful she was and told him all about Beech Hill. He still warned me to drop her.

But Jo wasted no time. She often had the young earl around when I was there; she also introduced me to a young man who was a professional charmer, running some business, and I wish had been running for his life. His charm was syrup. He seemed always to attach himself to any girl or woman with riches or publicity value. I certainly did not have the money, but I did have the glamour, so he attached himself to me. The only person who watched and saw what was really going on was the chauffeur.

After I had whittled down the number of creditors to less than half, I decided to join Edward for a few weeks on the island, as he was lonely and kept asking me to come. Getting to the west coast of Ireland is not easy, no matter how you travel, so why not a Cunard liner that called at Galway on her way to America? I went down to the Cunard offices in Regent Street and put my unique idea to Mr Kernan, the manager, who spun round in his swivel chair a few times. To his surprise and mine, he agreed to take us and put me, Bracken the spaniel and the chauffeur off at Galway.

The chauffeur was as excited as if he were going all the way to New York. It took us a day and a night, and every wave was higher than the last. He was sick, Bracken was sick and I thoroughly enjoyed myself and wished we could sail on to the New World. Then we got to Galway Bay and the tide was out and we couldn't get to shore! They had to hire a tender to fetch us, and even that got stuck in the mud, so a good time was had by all! Cunard will never try that again, nor will the people of Galway forget the unheralded arrival of their Premier Duchess, stuck in the mud, and on the Sabbath!

Edward was waiting, for hours I daresay, and felt like Dr Livingstone. As usual, he looked untidy but smiling. Well, poor fellow, he needed someone to look after him. Heather and Clover shouted with joy to see me, especially Clover, who was the noisy one. We all piled into the station wagon, which also needed a wash, and drove through that lonely, soft peat-smelling country to Renvyle in Connemara.

It was the country that got you. It always does, and when you go once, you always go back. We made it to the island by bailing out faster than you could count and there it was—the little white house that I had seen about a year before, with the stairs hanging on the outside. Inside was chaos and disorder, where Edward had passed his lonely hours, although some woman came from the mainland to cook and clean, if you could call it that, for Edward during his exile. Except for walks with the dogs, the flight of the swans, and watching the oyster catchers on the beach, there was little to do, except listen to Edward's collection of records of *The Ring*, which he played over and over again on a portable gramophone that he had got hold of. This I loved, and again learned the music and motifs of this great stirring opera from him, and a literal gift of the gods it was and always will be for me. On that lost little island I found my happiness, even though I wasn't really happy in myself. I got to know Brünhilde, Wotan, Siegfried, the giant gods and Loge, the god of fire, and such music that carried me to Paradise. For this I have Edward to thank and bless him for it. I think that he rather thought of himself as Siegfried, more sinned against than sinner. I think he had something there, for the one thing Edward was not, was a sinner.

I decided to go back to London to see how the wind was blowing and when it would be safe for Edward to follow. It was late September, the evenings were drawing in, and it was time to try to build our lives again. I took the chauffeur and went back to London, where I found a small service flat in Marsham Court in Westminster. From there I saw more creditors and got in touch with Jo Wessel, who was at the ready. She wanted to know, blow for blow, how it had gone in Ireland, and wanted to show me Beech Hill. Whenever she came to see me she was always dressed like a doll. She wore a bonnet, yes, a proper bonnet tied under her chin, and looked ready for the footlights. That baby doll use of her eyes made me giggle, but she had played it up so long as the 'Little Mishu' that it had become a habit. She was called 'Granny Bo Peep', and considered a rather dangerous joke, but I didn't get the message.

Edward came back when the majority of creditors had withdrawn their petitions. To be on the safe side, he went to stay with 'the Priest', where I joined him. He looked shabby and needed polishing up; I enjoyed doing this, for the result was so rewarding. When we went to this tailor in London, I took him to meet Jo Wessel, and that was the point of no return. This was what she had been waiting for. Edward still thought that she was 'bone common', as he put it, and not a suitable companion for me. How blind and dumb can you be, when she, who had proclaimed to all who knew her or had known her as Denise Orme, that she would die a duchess! I was just that blind and just that dumb.

Jo told me that she thought Edward was charming, but dull and not worth the sacrifice I was making. I deserved someone more my age who had a good life to offer me. I listened and saw her point, but it is my nature to stay the course, and I was deeply fond of my husband. Jo got us to drive her down to show us Beech Hill, which was pretty and done up throughout by herself. Edward didn't like it, but I thought any port in a storm was better than no port at all.

Meanwhile, I thought it prudent for Edward and I to go abroad until the dust had really settled, and have another honeymoon, our third, and last. We went to Kitzbuhl to ski and sit in the sun and wait until the coast was clear. Then Edward suddenly wanted to go to Vienna. I had never seen the waltzing city, so I was pleased to go. Edward said he wanted to show me pictures, the dancing white horses and take me to the opera. It sounded wonderful! We went to the Sacher, where we were called 'Herzog' and 'Herzogin', and treated as we should have been, had we been what we should. We had not been there an hour when the professional charmer I have mentioned rang our suite to say that he too was in Vienna and had heard that we were there. I must be off my rocker! How had he got there? And why?

This must be a joke call from London, but even that he could not afford. As Edward despised him, I suggested that we meet downstairs. To my increasing amazement Edward seemed delighted to see him, and suggested that we three see Vienna together! Nothing made sense. For three or four days we went about arm in arm—yes, Edward, the charmer and me—until I was so fascinated by this extraordinary, sudden relationship that I missed half the things I was taken to see.

One afternoon, when it was snowing and so still you could

hear the echo of your boots crunching in the snow, I went alone to the cathedral to pray for guidance, for not only was Hitler on the march, but so were my topsy-turvy thoughts. Never having seen Vienna when it was gay, it seemed the saddest, most doomed place I had ever been in. I was more than ready to leave when I got back to the hotel and found the inseparable Edward and the charmer anxious to do the same. Hitler was too close, and we had better get out while we could. Back to Kitzbuhl we went—not just Edward and I, but the charmer came too and brought a girl with him. When we got to Kitzbuhl, there were only two rooms at the inn, or so I was told. It was suggested that the girl sleep in the dressing room off my bedroom, and that Edward and the professional charmer share the other room for the night. I don't know which bedfellows were more cockeyed. I tried to think it was war on our heels; war it was, but this was my own private *Blitzkrieg*.

Never will I forget that crazy night as long as I live. Somehow it passed, for I dared not take my eyes off the Geisha wraith, and I wanted to get up and out of this trap. Trap it was! Edward had received a telegram to come at once to deal with a summons in London, and had already gone and left me alone with the charmer and the girl. To say nothing of Hitler!

I shook with panic and fury, sent a wire to Edward to meet me at Dover and got myself into a sleeper that night. One day later, Edward was at Dover, and three days later Hitler was at Innsbruck. What happened to the girl I don't know, but the charmer came up smiling.

Edward did meet me at Dover, having got the wind up, and really seemed relieved and happy that I was in his arms again and safe. He seemed so glad to see me that I really believed in the telegram to Austria and I really believed that Jo was after all our fairy godmother. She was trying to help, trying to help herself to a ducal coronet. She coaxed us into Beech Hill.

It didn't go well for us at Beech Hill. It was not a happy house, too full of plots and intrigue. No one had been happy in it, so we did not strike any roots. Instead of going to an hotel when we were in London, we went back to Marsham Court until I got ready a flat I took for us at Westminster Gardens, just across Horseferry Road. The Westminster Ice Rink was just behind the flat, and I used to skate there. I loved it and was learning to waltz on ice. Meanwhile we were getting settled into our pretty new blue flat with its small balcony and my long dreamed-of four-poster bed, high and soft like the princess and the pea. Then I got another ominous note from Edward.

This time he had gone for good, and to Jo! Would I please remove my things from Beech Hill and then disappear. It took a little while, for me at any rate, to feel the full force of the blow, especially when it was such a travesty as this. This creature, old enough to be Edward's mother, whom he warned me against and told me was a common bore—no, it was just not possible. But I had better collect my things from Sussex, as the house belonged to her.

The chauffeur, my maid and I drove down to Beech Hill, packed up my new clothes and possessions, including Edward's suits, and off we went to London. Less than a mile later we passed Jo, whose head was high, and Edward, whose head was low, indeed he ducked to the floor of the car in which they were driving when he saw me. Granny Bo Peep had won!

Mother came over from New York and I went all to pieces. I became ill and a white patch formed overnight in my bonnie brown hair from shock. I couldn't believe any of Edward's letter. It was his handwriting well enough, but the words and meaning were not. Dr Carey sent for him to come to see me. This he did, to my surprise and delight, but he would not stay with me. I never saw such a tortured and frightened soul. He was trapped.

When Jo's chauffeur came to collect Edward's clothes, it knocked me for six, but then I knew who was running this shoddy business. Poor Edward; he even came to see me when he thought no one was looking, and I gave him a small picture of me that he had had by his bed in Westminster Gardens. But when he finally left me, with the warmest and loneliest embrace, my picture did not go with him. He had come to ask me to divorce him, or rather he had been sent and told to do so, for he was as unhappy as I.

That was the last time he came, or almost, for after that he and Jo used to drive under my flat late at night to throw pebbles up at my window to see who would poke his head out. Yes, the same as the frame-up in Vienna. I had told the sordid story to a lawyer, but I was determined to delay taking any action for as long as I could to give Edward time to run for it.

So I went on with my daily life, listened to the pebbles at night as though they were rain and took myself in the car up to Scotland, where I had several invitations to stay. One was at Castle Leod at Strathpeffer, with Lord and Lady Tarbat, on my way to Elsick for a fortnight with Charles and Maudie, the Earl and Countess of Southesk, or rather Carnegie, as they were then.

My first visit was to a cold castle, charming to look at, but uncomfortable to stay in. My hostess was American, my host was the Laird of the West Coast, small, nimble and winning; he wore his highland dress with an air. From the moment I arrived at his castle door and for five years after, there was no doubt that he enjoyed being with me. He followed me wherever I went; to the Carnegies, the Guthries at Guthrie Castle, London, and the United States. I thought that it was all great fun and that he would tire; but he never tired, not when he was chasing a woman and I was that woman.

His wife laughed at his attentions to me, and so did his mother and so did Maudie and Charles, and indeed all of Scotland; but believe me it was no laughing matter, just grist to the mill for Jo and my poor unwilling husband. Discretion was not his lordship's middle name, and no one could possibly miss the hot pursuit of the viscount and the duchess bang in the height of the Scottish season. We danced all the reels, went to all the Games, in parties, and no one missed the romance of the year. His wife however, thought so lightly of it that she went to Sweden and left us together at his mother's house; when I saw that he really meant to have me and hold me for keeps, I went and told his mother and vanished in my car while he was fishing. But there was no turning back, at least not for him.

When I got back to London, the news had spread and detectives in cars followed me wherever I went. Jo and Edward were trying to force a quick divorce, but I would not touch it, as I preferred the devil I knew to the devil I didn't know. I wouldn't budge. Jo and Edward were living in Hamilton Terrace, in her house there, and at Beech Hill. They had Heather and my beloved Clover. But one day I came in from a luncheon to find my Clover tied to the towel rail in my bathroom. How did she get there? Edward had sneaked in while I was out, with the help of the head porter, to leave her there, and to take away a few things he had left behind in the rush. I had already been given Suki, a most adorable dachshund, by the professional charmer. She went everywhere with me: to the shops, click, click, click, with her nails on the pavement as she trotted behind me. If I left her in the car, she would stand with her hands on the window watching for me and looking like a little brown hammer. She went with me to Scotland, and even to the movies to see Pluto, whom she loved, and at whom she would growl. Clover used to sit on the box of the car next to the driver, as she used to sit there with her sister. She liked this and added to the smartness of the turnout. Suki preferred the back inside seat with me. We managed like this for a while.

Meanwhile my Scottish admirer was having his troubles with his wife, who had returned from Sweden, found that she had left the gate open and his lordship had lost his heart to another, and gone. What a muddle.

Then I was asked to attend the Opening of Parliament, and of all the grand and glorious sights I had hitherto seen, this was to me the most beautiful and moving of them all. In 1938, England's last year of peaceful splendour, I attended this impressive ceremony. In the Assembly Chamber were gathered the heads of governments, government officials, ambassadors and ambassadresses, peers and peeresses of the realm. At one end of the oblong Chamber were two little thrones on a dais. At the right of the thrones sat their Excellencies, the distinguished representatives of the Empire and other countries, looking very fine indeed in full Court dress and wearing their orders and decorations. On the left of the dais sat the ambassadresses, duchesses and peeresses in pale-coloured or white gowns, wearing long white gloves, tiaras and all the family jewels.

Mine consisted of Helen's blazing tiara and the splendid diamond brooch with the single emerald in the centre that she had given me on our wedding day. It hardly matched the magnificence of the rows of enormous emeralds on the neck of my beautiful neighbour, the Duchess of Buccleuch, but it added its sparkle to the general sparkle. In the centre of the Chamber were grouped the peers in their red robes, always worn on this traditional occasion. We all waited in our respective places for Their Majesties—my seat had my name in full on it when I arrived and it nearly frightened me to death.

All the lights were blazing, and so were the jewels. The trumpets were raised, a hush fell upon the house, and the fanfare sounded. We all rose and stood in silence. A second time the trumpets sounded, and slowly the brilliant chandeliers above us began to dim. As they faded, the thrones, which had until then been in darkness, began to glow softly with light. As they gained in brilliance and we were lost in darkness, the two slight figures of the King and Queen, wearing their magnificent crowns of State, moved through the doors and up and on to their thrones. There they turned and faced the Assembly, and the King delivered his speech, haltingly at times, but his gentle Queen would be ready and the touch of her hand on his arm steadied him. It was the most breathtaking sight, those two small figures standing side by side in all their simplicity and glory, and so human. It was all so sweet, so little, so big, so intimate and sincere, and had about it that fairy quality of beauty and importance, and the blending of yesterday, today and tomorrow.

From this exquisite scene, I returned in a daze to Westminster Gardens. I would have liked to stay alone to relive all that I had been fortunate enough to see, but my highland beau was on my heels, and so was Suki, wanting to go out. Still in my beautiful dress I put a coat round me to take Suki where she needed to go. Lord D. was with me when a strange man in a bowler hat and mackintosh came up to me and asked if I were me. I was so taken aback, as I did not know who he was, that I just looked at him. Then he asked Lord D. the same question, and before either of us knew what it was all about, we had been given a divorce summons, citing the Scot and the professional charmer as co-respondents! What an end to a perfect day!

I then instructed my lawyer to bring a case against Edward and Jo. Edward insisted that he was of Scottish domicile, so I decided to bring the case in Scotland, knowing that his domicile was England, and get it thrown out. This I did in Edinburgh, where I stayed at the Caledonian Hotel with my Gyppy, who came over from Malta to be with me again.

Lord D. was there too. He nearly had a fit because he knew that I had Dr Carey ready to go into the witness box to give evidence that would throw the case out. I had the proof that Edward had no Scottish domicile. So poor Lord D. was in a spin as we walked about the gardens of the courts. After all, he was still married, and I meant to keep it that way. One doesn't go about breaking up marriages, even if they are already broken. I was very fond of him, but I cared more for my husband than my partner in the petronella. How I loved that highland dance. He taught it to me and we used to dance it, the eightsome, and Strip the Willow at all the Scottish balls.

My divorce action stopped dead, and all the time in the world was on my side, which was what I was after. The Scot recovered from his depression, and hope sprang again in his fickle heart. We drove north and stayed on the way with friends of mine, who had taken the Chaplins' house for the shooting, and that was a visit that I will never forget. This nimble Scot was determined to marry me and let everyone see it.

Then on to Maudie, and back to London, and New York. I wasn't there ten minutes before the Scot showed up in a freighter. So what could a girl do? He took rooms round the corner from the Mayfair House, where I stayed and where mother and

Jimmie were. Dynamite wouldn't move him; but Hitler did. My friend Neville Chamberlain had been to Munich, and told us that there would be 'peace in our time', but only he was buying that. It was time to go back to England to see many things and how near or far we were to war.

There was a stillness in the air in London, but no peace in our time or anyone else's. Everyone seemed to be holding their breath even while they were holding forth on how impossible war was. Then Hitler invaded Czechoslovakia and Poland, and sabres were rattling everywhere. Then over the radio came the voice of Mr Chamberlain, so sad with defeat and the terrible announcement he had to make: 'I regret to have to tell you that we are at war with Germany.'

The blackout, the fingers of lights scanning the sky from dusk to dawn, the air-raid sirens, the deserted streets, and the complete change in our way of life. The Scot joined his regiment. Edward sent a message to see if I was all right, but he did not come. Uniforms appeared everywhere, and we got ready for the big bang. But it didn't come, and it didn't come, so we called it 'the phoney war'.

We all had to carry gas masks. One day when mine was hanging over my shoulder in its cardboard box I ran into Vic Oliver, the talented artist and conductor, in Asprey's. He said that I was much too elegant to carry my mask in such a box, and bought and gave me a very smart navy blue case for it, which I proudly wore. He also lived at Westminster Gardens, with his wife, Sarah Churchill. So did Jan Masaryk, with whom I made friends and whom I saw a lot of. He used to curl up in a chair and sit on his legs like a child, and talk and talk. He was a sad little man, and when we crossed to America on the same ship I learned of his sadness; how right he was, as history later proved.

I was very lonely and frightened there alone in Westminster Gardens. When the appeal was made for all Americans to leave, in my head I knew that I should go, for I would not only be another mouth to feed, but useless in a raid. If I hid in a cupboard in a thunderstorm, what would I be like when the bombs came crashing down? I would be a terrified liability and shame my rank and myself with cowardice. But in my heart I wanted to stay, for I loved this island, in spite of its indifference and insularity.

So I stayed on for a while until Lady Donegal, who lived in the flat under mine with her son Don, told me that I should go before it was too late. 'You have no ties here now, dear,' she said, 'and you can do much more for England in your own country than here.' She was right, as it turned out, for I would have died of fright long before I died from a bomb. I was no hero and Lady Donegal saw this, I am sure. Even so I stayed around, stumbling about in the blackout and waiting for the first raid that never came, to see if I could take it and be of some use.

Then came a message from the American Embassy telling me to go. The last ship would be leaving in five days' time and there was a berth left for me. I couldn't count the cables and telephone calls from mother, but I guess the American Ambassador could, so I agreed to go. I arranged for Harrods to pack up the flat and move all our things into store, on the off-chance that I would see them again when the war was over; we all thought it would be a matter of months.

Lord D. got leave of absence to drive me and Suki to Weston-super-Mare to wait there to sail in the American ship. I also took Maureen, the house-parlourmaid, with me. She was called 'the bog-trotter', for she was fresh from the Irish bog, with big feet and large eyes from which she stared at one and made one feel safe. She was young, fiercely devoted and wanted to come, so why not? I needed someone who was kind to look after me. How we got a place for her in the ship I can't remember, but maybe it was a hammock, for there were seven in my cabin and even more in hers!

The last night in England was grim. Suki and I waited alone in the uncomfortable hotel for my devoted Scot to deal with transport to the ship the following morning, as he had to leave at midnight. But to my surprise he did not leave me. Instead we did not sleep at all, but watched the long searchlights searching the night sky; we walked along the edge of the cliff above the bay counting the few hours that still belonged to England, for he too was going overseas. The day of parting had come.

We drove to the ship. When we got out of the car to go aboard her, Suki curled up on the back seat and never even looked up. She had been sad and quiet for several days, for she knew far better than I that we would never meet again. The Scot was to take her to Mary, Lady Delamere, from whom she came as a puppy, to stay with the butler, who loved her. But such was her love for me that she pined away three weeks after that heart-breaking day, right into her tailwaggers' heaven.

Fortunately, my friend Wylodine was also sailing in the last ship home. She had the awful pain of saying good-bye to the man whom she was going to marry, Brian. Up and down the pier we walked, the Scot and I, Brian and Wylodine, saying little, for what was there left to say that had not been said a thousand times? Only silent little Suki on the back seat of the car knew the ultimate answer and the agony in her small brown soul.

The whistle blew for all aboard. Wylodine and I had to bid farewell. We clung to each other as we went up the gangway and waved good-bye to two soldiers who loved us. We found it hard to get through the crowd to our cabin, which happily we were to share, but to our horror with five other strange women as well. The ship was packed with Americans like ourselves who had been told to go home.

She and I sat together on a lower berth, quite stunned. We said nothing until the whistle blew again for the last time. Then Wylodine flung herself into my arms with such force that she knocked the wind out of me. A most dreadful groan of woe rose from the two of us as our ship, painted with the stars and stripes from top to bottom and stem to stern, moved slowly and bravely out to sea.

Chapter 9

On that crowded journey I met Cecil Roberts, the writer, who very kindly mentioned me in his book *And so to America*. He explained that he, as English as he could be, was escaping because of his ulcers. I said that I was escaping because I was alone and scared. So he put me in his book to keep his ulcers company. When we got in to New York I got my first shock. They took my American passport away, clipping off the end of my British one so that I could at no time and in no way leave the land of the free and the home of the brave. I had completely burned my boats and, like Queen Victoria, I was not amused.

Wylodine went to Ohio and I went to Mayfair House with Maureen. I had a very pleasant corner flat there, high up on the tenth floor, where I was to stay far longer than I ever expected. It was good to be away from the blackout, which had got everyone down, and to eat again. Mother had found a room nearby for Maureen; all should have been well, but I felt like a fish out of water.

Everyone in New York was pro-British, or so it seemed. They were all worked up over helping the British and the crusade spirit was rampant. So far it was still a phoney war in Europe, and America was sitting back. Then came the terrible raids. Everyone wanted to do something. British War Relief was formed and money poured in from all over the country. Then came Pearl Harbor, and there was no looking back. We were *all* in it, and for six long and dreadful years.

Before this, I took Maureen and went to Canada to stay with the Urchin—the first Englishman who wanted to marry me when I was very young and green.

It took us four days and nights to get there in a train. I had a drawing-room from which I could sit and look out at the miles and miles of plains and trees, and trees and plains. The only happy relief was the prairie dogs. Never had I seen anything like them, nor will I ever forget their moment of happiness. Hundreds and hundreds of them lived in holes in the ground. One would come up and sit on his hind legs on top of his burrow and look and look and look, then he would raise his small face and let out a long, shrill, piping sound meaning 'all clear'.

Thousands of others would rush up from their tunnels and join in with the whistle. I couldn't get over this haunting, stolen moment of sheer happiness. There they were piping to their hearts' delight to the evening star. Fancy settling for that as their golden moment of life. It never lasted more than a minute, for some big bird or animal or snake would have them, but their stolen split second of joy piped to the moon taught me that all we really have in this grim and starlit world is the Now, and we must treasure it and enjoy it with all we've got and all we are, for it's gone in a jiffy. I will hear them, those brave little gophers all the days of my life, and be thankful, and whistle until it hurts. Try it—you will be surprised what it will do for you.

The Urchin met us and drove us to the Buffalo Head. Maureen and I settled into our crude huts and I was glad to be away on our own. I liked the small noises of animals on the roof at night and the cry of the coyote. I loved the sense of wildness, and soon made friends with the porcupine and bear who came sniffing at my door, and the little furry things that ran all over the roof, and the birds. We would rise with the sun and the Urchin would be ready with the horses; Molly for me, and Rex for him.

We would mount and gallop away like the wind. Oh how I loved the feel of the horse again and the freedom of it all. This was my kind of life, and I made the most of it. We would be out on the horses all and every day, riding twenty or thirty miles, making tea in a billy-can by a stream, and riding up into the hills to gaze at the vastness of this great big country. I can't believe it was I who got through the violent storms that came up out of a blue sky, in minutes. The roaring saffron curtain of hail stones that kill, that sent animals big and small rushing under any cover they could find . . . and me under the bed! And the lightning that danced on the mica in the foot-hills and split trees before you could get off your horse and dive under a tarpaulin.

The moose fascinated me. Big, ugly, clumsy looking animal, tall as a horse and as nimble as a gazelle. The cow with her calf could be seen feeding near the edge of a lake, for they ate the green under the water. But the bull! What a wonderful sight it was to see him running up the hill with his huge antlers, threading his way through the dense forest of trees at top speed and barely touching a leaf. Even if you could not actually see him, you could follow him with your eye by the path he wove through the pines.

The sky was electric blue and the many lakes like mirrors. Lake Louise was very beautiful, long and wide and full of whistling.

'What is it?' I asked. 'Sounds like the brave little prairie dogs.'

'Not dogs,' Urchin told me, 'but mink.'

Mink! And you pay fifty dollars just to look at a single skin in New York, and here they were in hundreds, whistling at you for nothing!

England had become home to me after so many years of growing up and living two married lives there. That small, misty, uncomfortable island of patch and mend gets in your blood and stays forever in your heart. Even though I could shake it and hit the smug, ungenerous, impersonal British over the head, I have learned so much from them, and wish that I could be like them. God knows I have tried, but after thirty years, I haven't learned a thing.

It was Lady Donegal who had told me that I could do more for England in America than I could have done had I stayed in London. I decided to set about trying to do just that, for

what roots I had were still there. I went to see Sir Godfrey
Haggard, Her Britannic Majesty's Consul General, and kins-
man of the writer, Rider Haggard. I took to him at once, for
he was an original, this tall, slim sandy-haired Englishman, with
a sense of values all his own, ready to laugh with you if he took
to you. I like to think that he did take to me, for we worked and
laughed together for many years, and shared a loyalty each for
the other when spiteful occasions arose, which they did more
often than not. Godfrey and his French-Canadian wife Geor-
gianna lived in a flat in Beekman Place. It ran the length of the
back of the building overlooking the East River, with a view of
little ships and sounds of the river traffic and Welfare Island.
Here I spent many happy hours with the Haggards and felt
that it was my reason and base for whatever I could do for
England.

British War Relief was an organization already in full swing,
and I went there to offer any help that I could give. When
'Bundles for Britain' was born I was offered the chairmanship
of the surgical division there. This I accepted and worked there
from the beginning to the end, well nearly the end, of the war,
when I had to fly back to England.

This organization was created by Natalie L., a born promoter
with tremendous energy and drive, who could persuade anyone to do what she wanted them to do and like it. Her little
girl voice, little girl looks and bubbling, boundless charm
brought them down like ninepins; she quickly collected a tremendous following and committees that more than matched
British War Relief. Yes, Natalie had more than it took to carry
them along with all their dollars, sympathy and support, while
emotion and devotion were the order of the day for the British.

I had an office tucked away at the back of the building.
Consequently it often happened that when visiting dignitaries,
such as the Duke of Windsor, whom I had met in London, came
with the Duchess to Bundles, they never saw the American with
the high British rank. But I was lucky enough to find a secretary
who was the best thing I ever came across in organization life.
Mrs McKenna was her name, a widow with two sons who lived

in Brooklyn and came over every day for five years to work with me. So quiet, gentle, wise and quick with shorthand, typing and filing, who saw how the whole place ticked from the start. Other heads of departments including Natalie, wanted her, but she would not budge, and how thankful I was, for I liked her enormously and could not have carried on without her.

My division had its own committee of twenty-three doctors chosen by the board and myself, and we were given acres of room in warehouses up on the West Side to receive all the surgical instruments and equipment which poured in from all over the United States. It was quite fantastic, the response from the generous, kind people from north, south, east and west of my own vast country of origin. I was stunned by it all and most deeply touched, for they believed in my adopted country as though it was their own, and any appeal that I sent out was granted a thousand-fold and immediately.

The instruments had to be sorted out and packed to go to England. Three nights a week doctors and nurses volunteered to come to the warehouses and do the sorting; they would work there until two and three o'clock in the morning, after having worked all day in their own offices and hospitals. We received operating tables, canteens, iron lungs, complete field hospitals, vaccines, oxygen tents—everything the helpful people of America could think of to send to Great Britain. And the stream didn't lessen with time. In fact, the more we were in the war together the more the dollars and instruments came, and Mrs McKenna and I had a busy time in our little back office.

Occasionally I was asked by our president to make a public appearance, either because she thought it prudent, or had something more important to do herself. Also there was always competition with the British War Relief, and maybe I could lend a little style to Bundles for Britain. So I lent a little style, and went to Philadelphia to a ball, representing Great Britain. A dinner was being given by a Mrs Clothier and I was their star turn. During the dinner I was warned that there was a lot of anti-British feeling about and that I might be picketed, so we must allow plenty of time to deal with the situation should it arise. Knowing that I had been let out of my box to do my stuff as a duchess, I dressed myself up in grand style for the evening and wore my long diamond chandelier earrings. When we drove up to the entrance of the hotel where the ball was to be held, sure enough, there they were, walking up and down, up and down, carrying placards with 'Down with Britain', 'Down with the Duchess' on them. Well, I thought, I'll go down in good company! The police were holding back the 'angry crowds' that I had been told to expect, but they looked to me more interested in what I was wearing than where I was going. My hostess was fearful for me as I stepped out of her shining Cadillac, only to be greeted by a rousing cheer! This surprised her and all her party; they loved drama, as do most Americans, and this reception was not what they had expected at all. Then one of my earrings fell off. That did it and made my evening!

The young man who had been carrying the placard saying 'Down with the Duchess' flung it aside, dropped to his knees on the new red carpet rolled out for the occasion, and began to search for it. 'Here it is!' he shouted with excitement, and rose with a smile all over his good-looking face and handed me my earring. 'It's awful pretty,' he said, '. . . and so are you.' As I thanked him and put on my earring, England and I got a tremendous ovation as we made our way to the door. I did all right too at another quite different ball in New York.

We were all taken to a masonic hall to the Caledonian Ball to dance reels and whoop it up to such a Scottish pitch that no one knew or cared who was from the Highlands and who was from Brooklyn. However, on this very amusing night, I met Tommy Emmet, whom I had seen vaguely on the *Manhattan* during our crowded, uneventful voyage from Weston-super-Mare to the safe shores of our own country. What a beautiful thoroughbred! Tall, elegant and soigné, with the face of a saint. As I said, I had noticed him on the ship, always hovering near an even taller young man who was obviously his brother. He too had beauty, but there was something wrong there, obviously a breakdown, and Tommy was indeed his brother's keeper. We never met on the ship because of his brother's illness, but happily we did meet on this crazy night, and thirty years later I consider him my dearest friend.

Tommy is the direct descendant of Robert Emmet, the Irish patriot who led the Irish Rebellion with my famous ancestor by marriage, Lord Edward FitzGerald. Quite a coincidence, and indeed a lucky one. Tommy resembles the statue of Robert Emmet in Dublin so much that he could well have posed for it. He lives with his family in a tall, white, colonial house high up on a cliff looking over Long Island Sound, caring for his old distinguished mother, his brothers and sisters, and many exotic birds. He knows all about God and His angels, and tried to dedicate his life to prayer by becoming a monk, but he had not the health for such rigours. He had to leave his holy order and later he lost a lung.

There was also that call to pomp and circumstance that I too had heard and followed, that drew him as it had drawn me. He knew all about that too—who everyone was, who was related to whom, kings and princes by the score. So he found himself a beautiful Austrian princess and married her.

Mrs Robert Bingham, widow of the former American Ambassador to England, was appointed head of Bundles for Britain. Just at this time I wanted to send money I had collected and promised to hospitals in London, and there was little to send! That blew the lid off, and there was a row you could hear rattling round the stricken world. I was not too surprised, for it was a costly operation, but Mrs Bingham and the twenty-three doctors on my committee were more than a little baffled and angry. It was a tough corner for all, especially for me, as it was I who had collected and made promises, and now it looked as though I had lost my donors. It was very embarrassing for the incoming and outgoing presidents, and once again the duchess became the whipping boy.

You can keep organization life from what I've seen of it. It's often the home and opportunity for prima donnas and social climbers, a jungle of personalities jockeying for place, the first place, and the cause is the platform. Thank God for my small back office, my unobtrusive, splendid secretary, Mrs McKenna, the twenty-three loyal and helpful doctors on my committee, and for the trust and generosity of the American people. Never was I more happy to be a back bencher than when Britain's Bundle came undone and spilled its bag of tricks. However, there was one good thing that came of it: Michael Coleman from a bombed All Hallows in England walked in out of the blue. First into Natalie's office, then happily into mine.

What a vital, magnetic young man he was! Strong, alive, with dark good looks and an appeal that drew people to him like flies. Wherever and whenever he spoke there was never an empty seat even an hour before he appeared. Men as well as women stood in the aisles just to listen while he fired them with his words and his gift of using them to cast a spell. I could feel the power of his presence the moment he came into my cubicle and delighted in his forceful personality and drive. We became friends immediately, and took it from there. His sex appeal was part of his charm and he knew it, and so did I. He also had a following few priests get, except Father Vernon, who christened me in London when I was old enough to want it myself!

Michael had a shy, reticent, gentle little wife and two children. He brought them to see me and we talked and talked, he and I. I gathered that he and Tubby Clayton, Vicar of All Hallows, had worked together through the Blitz. Michael would never bend to anyone's will, not Clayton's, nor Natalie's either, who liked him immensely, as we all did. He was a leader and must be treated as such.

I had the idea that he should speak to the Archbishop of Canterbury from a cathedral pulpit in the USA at an Intercession Service to which all who represented, prayed or worked for Britain should come, and this service should be broadcast to the world. This brainwave came to me in the night, and the next day I told Michael. He was enthralled, and so was I. I went at once to see the Head of Churches and told my story. When I told him that I wanted St Patrick's Cathedral for

Michael, he spun round and looked at me to see if I were mad. I said: 'Why not? "In my House are many mansions." '

A smile spread over his face like the sea coming in, and he said, 'Why not? At least I'll know where to come whenever I want the impossible accomplished.' 'You too have the aura of the leader,' he told me.

Well, had I? At least such a remark from such a man gave me the courage I sadly needed to try my luck, for when I do something for someone else I believe in it because I believe in them. For myself I can do no good at all.

Americans were proud of the wise, friendly little Archbishop Spellman, as he was then, who always said the right and kind thing. I'd have a go at him and see. An appointment was made for me to go to the archbishop's house at the back of St Patrick's in Madison Avenue. It was pouring with rain, and when I rang the door bell an old butler let me in and led me to a high, stiff red plush chair. I hoped that he would take my dripping umbrella, but he didn't, and the puddle got bigger and bigger as I waited.

Presently a little round man with a little round scarlet cap on his round head and a blazing scarlet sash at his middle came to fetch me, to take me to the archbishop, I thought. He led me into the drawing-room, which was full of more stiff, red plush chairs and Victorian lace curtains, and I still had the streaming umbrella! I presumed that this little man was taking me to His Grace, but he made no further move, so finally I held out the umbrella for him to take it, believing that this was what he was waiting for. He immediately took it and went peeking behind table and chairs looking for a place to put the wretched thing.

'Let's come in here and have a little talk,' he said. We sat down side by side on a large, hard, horsehair sofa, and then I noticed his ring! Heavens, this cosy little man was the archbishop, one of America's greatest ambassadors of peace, to whom all genuflected and kissed the rings of office. And all I had done was to hand him a dripping umbrella!

I told him what I had in mind for Michael, and he listened

with interest and full attention. 'Some day,' he said, 'some day, but not yet. He is not a priest of Rome.' How right he was, for now so many doors are open to all faiths that were closed then. I am glad that he lived to see it happen, for behind his spectacles his inscrutable eyes saw far beyond the horizon.

He told me to carry my message to the vicar of another cathedral, this time a church of Michael's faith. There I went to see this man of God, who was as cold to my suggestion as the archbishop had been warm. He had heard about Michael and his tremendous popularity and success, and he was certainly not going to further it. My visit with him was brief and chill, and I saw at once that he would not encourage a visit from someone like Michael, not for one hour in his pulpit, no matter what the cause.

So I was soon dismissed and went back to Mayfair House with bitter thoughts. CBS were ready to broadcast the hook-up. I had told my story to Helen Sioussat, who was head of the department that dealt with such talks. She was all for it and had laid it all on, while the Archbishop of Canterbury, Dr Fisher, was ready and waiting for dates.

The British Ambassador, he was the man. Lord Halifax, surely he would find a welcome pulpit for Michael to spread his message of grateful thanks and England's need together with the Archbishop of Canterbury, who stood, as Churchill did, for England's finest hour. Of course, a religious man of vision as Lord Halifax was saw it all in a flash. Before you could count to ten, it was done: the Washington Cathedral, fit for a pope, was offered by the Bishop, and dates fixed. What a great occasion it was! Loudspeakers were posted all round outside the cathedral for the thousands who could not get in to hear the service. There was no room inside the cathedral which was packed to the doors with representatives of all nations and British organizations. The bells rang as we entered, Michael, standing there in the pulpit looking as though he had been touched by God.

It was arranged that all the ambassadors and distinguished guests should be seated in the choir, with Her Royal Highness

Princess Marthe of Norway. Lord Halifax read the lesson, and then we all stood rapt in silence, listening to the voice of England from across the sea. I think if people could cheer in church they would have done so, for the atmosphere was charged with emotion and joy. Some knelt and wept. Outside when it was over the people burst into song: 'There'll always be an England'. Inside and out the organ pealed 'God Save the King', and the bells rang like on New Year's Eve.

What a day, what an occasion, what a glorious success! All that Michael and I had dreamed of and more, much more. The whole world had heard, and the whole world had listened, for the power of right is far greater than might, and always will be.

We had another Intercession Service at St Bartholomew's in Park Avenue, and the people were standing right out into the street. Then Michael went to Canada, and on to Vancouver, where he took a living and became Bishop Qu'Apelle. He is still there I believe, carrying his cross to those who thirst.

Before we went to Washington for the Great Day, I had met at a supper at the Waldorf Towers, a man of exceptional attraction and vanity: Charles McCabe, the publisher of the *Daily Mirror*. The supper was given by Mrs Chandler, aunt of Tommy Emmet. She was a fascinating woman and had many admirers. Charles was one of them. I was placed next to him at supper, and from that night in the clouds we became friends and almost lovers. I say almost, because he had a wife and family of whom he was very proud, and I had had my experiences with Lord D., and knew that it could only lead to disaster for all concerned. As I look back, I often wish that I had been more heartless, for we had something that I for one have never found again; for a man as vain as Charles, once rejected, never returns.

He was thrilled by my service in Washington, and sent me a cable that would make any woman's heart sing. He wanted me to have a radio news programme of my own on Hearst Network! Charles was Prince Charming indeed and gave me the chance of a lifetime. After our happy meeting in the sky, he asked me to lunch a few days later and told me of his idea of a radio programme for me. I was rapt with attention and the pleasure of his charming self. He told me that I would have to have a sponsor to buy me and put me on the air, and had just such a man ready and waiting to meet me!

American newspaper men certainly waste no time, and when they get a bee in their bonnets they jolly well let it buzz. I had never spoken over the air and dreaded every occasion when I had to address a meeting or a gathering. I was shaking in my boots at the thought of becoming a radio commentator. But not a minute was lost. The very next day Charles had Charles Skouras to lunch to meet me, having completely sold him the idea. Before I had finished my coffee I was whirled up to WINS for a test and bought and paid for within the hour. I was dizzy with excitement and misgivings. I hadn't a clue. Who would start me off? Charles' assistant helped me with the first two scripts and I was put on at one o'clock for ten minutes to give me the feel of it.

I loved it, and in fact had no mike fright. I was introduced as Mrs Edward FitzGerald with 'The News behind the Real News'. No one could see me and no one knew who I was. This was my idea of bliss, and away I went for two long years, twice a week at nine o'clock at night with my own announcer and fifteen minutes to talk to America. If people can't look at pictures of what is going on, they like to hear them, and I had all the pictures, because I knew many, many of the men and women who were making the news at home and overseas in the war. But what I needed, indeed had to have, was an assistant who was well-informed, well-read and highly educated, who could do the research and supply accurate information. I had none of these qualities. I had the touch and could put it over, but fifteen minutes is a long time and needed seven pages of informative, well-padded and topical material to get and hold the audience.

Luck was with me. I found Mr Winter, a young man with all the qualities I sought and more. He worked with Pepsi-Cola, and I think is now their president. If not, he should be. We hit it off at once. On his way home from work every night he would call in to see me at Mayfair House to discuss the topics of the day and what I would like to talk about the following evening. The idea was to dramatise and humanise the news. We broke it down into three subjects. Having got the swing of it, Winter would go home and draft it all out in his own dry but precise words and leave it the following morning for me to rewrite in my own words. I had to feel sure of my ground, for we, or rather I, was tapped by all information services from all countries and had to be right. Being the amateur that I was, I found that I could put it across in my own words, but got all tangled up in someone else's.

Anyway, it worked and I had two scoops, was cut off the air three times and collected quite a following and more fan mail than I could deal with. Those two years were the most useful of my life, and an experience I would not have missed for anything. The days and nights flew with the work, for no sooner did I come off the air than I had to prepare to go on again.

The immeasurable help and kindness of the professional news analysts, such as Raymond Gram Swing, William Shirer, Edward R. Murrow, Fielding-Eliot, and several others, and of course Helen Sioussat, was in itself something to try to live up to. The technicians and my announcer were my team; I worked with them as one, and loved them for it. They showed the greatest humour and patience the night one of my pages went skating to the floor and I went down under the table to get it and it skidded further away! I went right on talking, telling my audience—if I still had one—just what I was doing, and my announcer wasn't the same man for weeks after that.

It was fun from the beginning to the end. It was hard work too, and I did not leave New York for one single week-end, except for the Fourth of July. Then I listened to a play-back while I was supposed to be on the air, and the needle got stuck and I kept saying 'and over the they river went . . over the river they went', five times until I wished that 'they', whoever 'they' were, would drown, to say nothing of my boring self sitting up in Cape Cod.

I saw a lot of Charles McCabe, to our mutual delight. I also had my problems with a couple of Greeks. One especially, another tall, sad, bony and intense type, was going to get me if it killed him. It nearly did, for he just couldn't take 'No' for an answer, and when the inevitable big pounce came, after weeks and weeks of stalking me, I had to hit him hard. Even then he didn't get the message, but I saw to it that we met only in the office and when the other Greeks were there!

What a contrast to Charles, who was gay and smiling, so gentle and a wonderful friend. It was unbelievable what he did for me when a nondescript man in a mackintosh came into the Bundles office and asked for me, saying that he had a summons to serve me with. Round he was sent to my office, where Mrs McKenna and I were busy at work, and handed me a petition for divorce by my husband! I couldn't believe what I saw or heard, and took the wretched paper. Needless to say, all the workers were agog, and wanted to know what it was all about. No one wanted to know more than I, so I rang Godfrey Haggard immediately. He told me to come to him at the consulate at once, to do or say nothing to anyone, certainly not to the chap in the raincoat.

Dear Godfrey, he was as upset as I was, only furious rather than emotionally wounded and frightened. He rang the embassy in Washington and asked them to recommend the best solicitor they knew of in England to represent me. It was not easy when the bombs were falling all over that country. Apparently Edward had established domicile in England. He was living in a caravan at Beech Hill, so I heard, with Jo in the house, to make it look innocent, and they were using the same faked-up evidence that they had produced before when I had it thrown out at Edinburgh when I proved that Edward had no Scottish domicile, and I was told by a lawyer that it could never be used again. Presumably he meant in Scotland. However it was being used again, and the hearing date was fixed! What do you do when you have no passport, and you can't get back to defend?

The service of the summons was only part of the attack.

Simultaneously, a thirty-word cable of certain accusations was sent to the *Daily Mirror*. It was addressed to the gossip columnist, but by the grace of God it got to Charles. He rang me at once, told me about it and said that I could use it in any way I wanted and he would support me. He told me that he was horrified by the contents, but more so by the person who had sent it. I then told him what had happened at Bundles and he was on his way before I could hang up. I will never forget his sympathy, kindness and constant support during the weeks that followed. He was so wise, true, and even more generous with his white orchids (always white) and his loyal attentions.

I loved him for it, for after all he was a newspaperman and could have published a story about me that would have sold millions of copies and done me irreparable harm, even though none of it was true. But Charles was a man if ever there was one and a very remarkable one indeed. Instead, he published a story about me that I have spent the rest of my life trying to live up to. And those who read it and those who saw the summons served smiled upon me with a warmth and respect to which I had hitherto been unaccustomed.

All this happened in our third office, opposite the library on Fifth Avenue, before the big change-over of presidents, before the borrowing from my fund to pay expenses, and long before Lord Halifax walked up the aisle of the Washington Cathedral at Michael's service, with neither Bundle on his arm—to both presidents' dismay.

There must have been gnashing of teeth at Beech Hill when the trick didn't work. They were a charming pair, the caught and the ruthless, who would stop at nothing to get a duke—not even a war. Jo's trump card was the fact that I could not get back to defend, and that the two so-called co-respondents were on active service overseas and couldn't get back either. I counted on time and events, and got a postponement. I could either agree not to defend, let the case go through, and be made the guilty party, or divorce him. I could play for time and go back as soon as Mrs Shipley, the queen of passports in Washington, would either give me my American passport and a visa, or allow me to use my British one. She wouldn't give either, not then, and I wasn't sorry, for it was an excuse that held.

If, however, I fought and won, I would be stuck for the rest of my life with my husband and I had taken quite a beating from my marriage. In spite of my deep affection for him and making allowances for his guileless character, I was not as sure as I had been that I wanted to take a high dive right back into the bottomless pit.

I will never forget those nights of torment in my corner bedroom in Mayfair House, thrashing back and forth; should I? shouldn't I? with mother aiding and abetting with her indecision, frightened talk, and love for a fight—any fight—just so long as she won. Perhaps she was right, but what if I did win? Round and round we went. And the cables! We must have sent a hundred. Never was I more grateful for anything than my work and the goodwill and presence of Charles McCabe.

What a wonderful friend he was to me, but I wanted it to stay that way. He loved his pretty wife and two sons and was very proud of them. I needed him for the dear friend that he was—I had been responsible for breaking up one marriage and it must never happen again. So I let him go, and I shan't ever forget those three days and three nights of silence that followed our parting. They have remained between us for ever more.

After nearly two years of seeing him, I found it mighty hard to take. Was I right, or just a mug? His interest in my radio programme went with him and I soon got lost in the shuffle. I might have gone far in broadcasting, and earned my keep, had I been the woman I never was and grabbed a good thing when I found it. Even to this day I don't know whether I was right or just a fool.

Chapter 10

There was another kind of fire burning in mother's flat, five floors below mine in Mayfair House where I would go and sit on the evenings when I was not out dancing on the town. The searing fire of discontent and humiliation. How could two people live together in two rooms with neither respect nor affection for each other and no love at all? Jimmy, my mother's third weak and ineffectual husband, was tall, good looking and caught up in a world he was neither brought up to nor wanted to be in . . . and the loser.

Mother met him in Stamford and married him. He had a good responsible job as Chief Accountant at The Yale and Towne Company, was well liked for his quiet ways and was highly respected locally. No sooner had she married him than she decided that he should leave this job and go to work for A. J. Nutting & Co in her father's firm in Brooklyn . . . which he wanted to do not at all.

I was too young then to heed the warning. Mother was still a sacred word. I was rammed down my stepfather's throat. 'My daughter this', 'my daughter that', 'my daughter, my daughter' until he came to hate me and who could blame him. He was dragged to Europe, to England not once but twice, to follow me and my antics, when all he wanted to do was to sit on a bench in his own home town and smoke his cigar and watch the world go by.

This kindly, gentle man never complained, just obeyed, then illness took its toll. Into hospital he went and nearly did not come out at all. When he did it was with little if anything left inside, except an even more saddened heart. For he could not work again, not even at the job he hated. He was entirely dependent upon mother, who found it all a great strain . . . so she got a nurse (from yet another advertisement in the newspaper), who was an ageing down-and-out. A 'Yes' woman of course, a Miss Barrow, who was obliged to sleep in a chair with a long string tied to her toe, so that mother or Jimmy could pull it in the night if they wanted anything! This grim situation went on for five years!

Finally mother, who could bear it no more, sent Jimmy to a distant farm in Pennsylvania, which I am sure she thought was the best thing to do. For one long desolate year he stayed there quietly waiting and just as quietly he died.

As I have said, I was too young, spoilt and self-centred to realize the far-reaching effect this situation would have upon my own future. This was indeed the shattering time of awakening but even though I knew it existed I had not become fully aware of it.

Perhaps this setting of bitterness and—oh—such loneliness— is what clipped my wings, for I have no self-confidence, am always out of my depth and dare not fly too high. Like the lark I hover in mid-air in a safe spot.

Was this ruthless need to rule caused by fear in my tiny mother? Or was it, as I like to think, a lack of humour and sense of fun? Surely almost anyone can live with almost anyone if they can laugh together—at each other and at themselves. It is the sunshine of life and if you can't laugh long, loud and often, well, you are better dead.

The whole of Mayfair House seemed filled with hatred and foreboding and I was so pleased when I was asked to go to Palm Beach. I was put up at the Brazilian Court Hotel, which was charming; my hostess and her family were also staying there. Invitations poured in for them, and many included me. I have never been to so many parties in my life. I never once saw the sea, which was one of my main reasons for going there, as well as for the pleasure of being with my hostess and her sister, who was then married and busy with her own friends. No sooner would one go out in one dress than one returned to change and go out in another. Happily, I had a few dresses that I liked to choose from, and this was fun for a few days and nights, for it never stopped as long as I was awake.

When would I get into the sea, or even see it? This was too much! So was the crack in the gossip column about me and a young man, who was a friend of my hostess, that caused quite a stir. Not a pretty stir, and his mother was heard to say unkind things about me. I wanted to get away. That very night when tongues were in full cry, there was a dinner being given for me at the Everglades Club. I had to walk in smiling as though the world were mine, but I dreaded it. Then my zip stuck! Zips may be the answer to a woman's prayer, but not on this occasion. What do you do when you are alone and you have got yourself into your most glamorous dress, and can't move the wretched thing up or down?

It was ten o'clock, and the dinner was at nine-thirty! I put my stole round me, picked up my bag and gloves, and off I went for better or worse. I didn't dare breathe in or out, but I held my head high and walked into that gathering as though I had been properly zipped into my beautiful black lace from head to foot by the maid I no longer had. I apologized for being late, to find that I wasn't late at all, for Americans stand for at least an hour drinking cocktails before they sway in to dine.

I got myself into the powder-room, where the maid got the engineer to deal with the zip, with a pair of pliers. A yank and a pull and it was as good as new. I don't think anyone knew that I had arrived completely undone in every sense of the word.

Having already made my entrance, I was even more nervous at rejoining the forty or more guests, knowing that they were discussing me. But dinner was served at long last and my host came to take me in. There were two great tables in the garden lit by tall silver candelabra, with dozens and dozens of red roses down the centre of each. I was bowled over by the

137

lavish abundance and expense of it all, for here ration cards were unheard of. I was seated beside Mr Brokaw, who was being extremely kind and attentive, which warmed me, for I was very ill at ease, and he knew it. Towards the end of dinner he suddenly got up, to my surprise, and went to fetch the young man's mother. They returned and stood by my side and he introduced her to me. What a generous, observant man my host was, and it was rather brave of her, whom I found charming. Dinner ended at midnight on a happier note than it had begun, and I returned to the Brazilian Court zipped up and smiling.

The following day was indeed one to remember. Edna wanted me to go with her to a luncheon that was being given for the Oxford Group, now called Moral Rearmament. I had heard of this group, not too favourably, and went with mixed feelings.

Dr Buchman was the head, and his followers were earnest young men, and conscientious objectors—some well-known personalities from different walks of life, one of whom I sat next to at one of the several small tables. They were on tour in the United States in Cadillacs and given shelter and food by the richest widows in the land, and were saving the world and enjoying it in the sun. Not a bad way to get through the war. Not bad at all!

I asked my neighbour a few leading questions, all of which he answered when he rose to address the guests. I felt that he had been asked them all before and had learned the answers by heart. Effective, but not convincing. His speech was really to introduce Dr Buchman with a flourish, which he needed from this fair-haired youth—for Dr Buchman looked anything but a leader.

Here we sat, in the middle of a war, in the middle of a pseudo-Spanish castle, surrounded by lawns, terraces and palm trees in Florida, and countless old and middle-aged millionaire ladies who were lapping up every word and loving it. It was fantastic and completely unreal.

Then Dr Buchman stood up and proceeded to read a poem

that he had written to the hostess! It wasn't true, but then none of it was. Wait until you hear what followed.

He said, 'We are gathered here today to bless the new swimming-pool of our dear hostess.' He then poured orange-juice from a silver jug, invoking the blessing of almighty God—when someone dropped a small wreath of orange blossoms with a p-l-o-p! which promptly sank! You could have heard my laugh in Hawaii—which I pretended was a sneeze!

But after twelve nights and days of dressing up and little or no sleep, I was so exhausted that I sent myself a telegram to come home. I had my work to return to in New York: also another beau, who was a delight to be with and to look upon. Most of the men in my life were feckless, but they all had something to recommend them: either style, looks and charm, or the elegance of rank. My eye for beauty and style led me to put my faith in princes. I never had the 'in between beaux' times. There was always someone hanging about, anxious to prove his skill. With Alec Telfer-Smollet, an old and merry colonel from Scotland who had made a bit of history for his country in his gallant command of the International Defence Forces in Shanghai, it was easy going. He was a widower and faced with retirement in the vastness of his romantic place, Cameron, on the banks of Loch Lomond. Perhaps a young wife would help to while away the years, sitting there watching the view? Perhaps I would jump at the chance, as I have always loved Scotland and the Scots, and wanted a home above all else in the world. But his nature to laugh with you and at everything saved that awkward situation. Later on, when the war to end all wars was over, I went to Cameron for a very gay visit, and found there his two sons, Patrick and Michael, who became and still are my friends.

There was another beau, David Pleydell-Bouverie who had a ranch in California called The Valley of the Moon! He was full of laughter and a spinner of moonbeams who sent me primroses saying 'For this moment or eternity'. Then he married

Alice Astor, who not long after left this world for the valley of eternal night instead of the Valley of the Moon.

There were merry times and worrying times, especially in mother's flat in Mayfair House. The only happy thing mother did was to give me very early meals the two nights a week that I had my programme. I found it better to eat sometime before I went on the air at nine o'clock. She was also helpful in finding interesting material. Seven pages twice a week needed more than just facts, and fifteen minutes without a break was quite a lot of talking. No sooner had I come off the air than I would have to prepare the next programme. When I think of the two years of dark nights I used to stand out in the street outside the studio, waiting for a taxi to take me home, with no fear at all. Even mother, the fearmonger, never thought twice about it. But now, one would not dare to set foot outside the door!

I would listen to the deep minor notes of the *Queens*, especially the *Mary*, calling to me from the river as they came and went, and that quickened my heart and made me homesick for England.

The battle for time in the divorce overseas, my awful indecision, my dwindling jobs and my own family situation nearly finished me. Surely anything was better than this. There was nothing I could do about it. The best thing was to leave it. So when I met Mrs Winant, the wife of the American Ambassador in England, I asked her if she could get her husband to tell Mrs Shipley to let me go back to England, as I had a divorce case to defend.

I had to face the music in England. I had been spared the bombs and horrors of war and had come home to mother. Now I must go home from mother, and make a life in another place. Four or five years I had spent in my own land. They had been filled with interest, work and play. I had danced through every ballroom and been called the 'waltzing duchess'. I had twirled a measure in the Vanderbilt mansion where 'the duchess', as Mrs Neeley was affectionately called, held court. We were two of a kind in a way. One wore a headache band, the other strawberry leaves, both crowns of thorns.

I had also got to know frail Marjorie Morowitz, who enter-
tained the world in her palatial apartment in Seventy-Ninth
Street. Here I met Jalmar Procope, the Finnish Ambassador;
he never missed a pretty woman, even though his wife outshone
them all. He didn't miss me either, and I learned about diplomats from him! Then there was Peggy De Gripenberg, wife of
the Finnish Ambassador to London, who spread her hospitable
wings over all and sundry, which, I found out to my surprise,
was as much a personal need as a warm and generous act.
She was a worker and a collector of persons, but her distinguished handsome husband George, sitting somewhere alone
in Sweden, was the puzzle. How could she leave him for even
a minute?

The call to England was still in my heart. Mr Winant had
waved the wand and Mrs Shipley was at last sending me an
American passport. My English lawyer, recommended by the
British Embassy in Washington, was expecting me and the
hearing of my case had been postponed, owing to the pressure
of work, lack of judges in wartime, and the fact that I had been
unable until now to get back. So all was ready and waiting
three thousand miles away for me to get transport and get there.
That took a bit of wangling, for only military personnel, VIPs
and members of the government were allowed to travel. Mr
Winant arranged this too. I was to fly in a seaplane as a VIP
back to the land of my choice, to no one—neither close friend,
relative nor home—to try to make of it what I could. The
uprooting and leave-taking was a pain, not unlike my first big
one long ago when my adorable wall-eyed Daisy died with her
head in my lap. I hurt inside and out and wanted to cry every
hour on the hour. How hard it was to grow up and to walk
alone, and fly alone, for I had never been in a plane in my
life.

VIPs, I was told, and I was one of them for the first time
since I had left the sceptred isle, so the plane would be full of
top brass and people in high places. I expected to see medals
and briefcases and faces that made news. When I walked up the
gangway of the wallowing whale heaving about in the Bay, I

felt dejected and needed a smiling friendly face to help me on my solitary way. What did I find? One seat for me and the rest of the entire aircraft filled with Jewish salesmen. Not a medal, not a uniform, not a briefcase, nor a face that I had ever seen before or wanted to see again. All men, all frightened, as I noticed when we began to fasten our seat belts and churn our way for take-off.

This time ignorance was bliss, for I had never been in a plane before and I thought it very exciting. I would have hung out of the windows if I could have done so, as I didn't want to miss any of it. How fast we were going on the small bit of water! Would we ever make it before we hit something? Then, with a tremendous lunge and spray of water, up, up and away we went into the sky. How wonderful, I thought, and turned to my companion to share the fun. He was hanging on to a paper bag and wished I would shut up and go away. So I got up and went as far away as one can in the air, only to see that most of the other passengers were in the same condition! What a bore I must have been, enjoying every minute of the flight, and the only woman among them. Happily, I had a window seat and never missed a cloud. The colours, the sense of space, and the beauty of it all kept me interested and able to forget what I had left behind me. Then we were told to fasten our seat belts as we were coming in to land and refuel at Newfoundland.

Again I was thrilled, especially when I looked down and saw the tiny lake on which we were to land. It was the size of a half a crown! The nearer we got the smaller it got, until I was bracing myself with my feet pushing hard against the seat ahead of me. It just wasn't possible to hit that tiny target. I didn't dare to look at my neighbour; I could feel his panic. Then a mighty wallop, and the whole lake seemed to cascade over us! I was riveted with exhilaration and pressed against the window to see as much as I could through the waves! I wanted to shout with glee, but I didn't think my queasy fellow passengers would be at all amused. The dripping craft came to a halt and we were told to get out and stretch our legs. I took a good look at the great hulk as she rode the little waves while she was being serviced, and I couldn't believe that she had been up there in the sky with all of us in her.

We went into the terminal to pass the time and soon we were told to board the aircraft for take-off again. I got even more of a kick out of it the second time, and when we landed with the same terrific splash in England, I was sorry it was over. I have never enjoyed a flight to this day as much as that one, for I hadn't a qualm or the slightest sense of danger.

And what a day to arrive! V Day, and the whole of England was dancing in the streets! This soon included all my fellow passengers, crew and myself. The war was over, even the doodle-bugs had stopped, and England, who had stood alone and lost the flower of her country, rejoiced and flung hats in the air. The whole of London was bedlam. I had been spared the real war and returned on the day of peace. My guardian angel must have timed it so, for none of us had a clue that it would happen that day.

It was quite a drive from our splashdown to the Dorchester Hotel, to which I returned from habit and from choice. It took more than an hour to make our way through the long-suffering victorious people of London. The traffic-lights meant nothing, and it was sheer luck that a taxi was found to get me to Park Lane from the terminal, after the wild ride in the bus from the airport.

When I finally arrived at the hotel, there waiting for me was the solicitor whom the British Embassy in Washington had selected to take my case. I had almost forgotten the highly civilized charm and good looks of the Englishman until I saw Philip. We had a few words together, and arranged to meet the following day. 'Come and lunch,' he said. I knew then that I could win my case with this man, no matter what the odds.

Up to my eyrie of seven years ago. There it was, pretty much as I had left it, on the top floor with a view of St Paul's. Cool and quiet with a bathroom big enough to waltz in. My spirits rose. I was back in England. I was on my own and the war was over. What a time to return! The luck of the Irish indeed! Before I left my room with a view again it had quite a story to tell about those who came to tell it.

Philip, my handsome lawyer, had applied for postponement of the hearing of my case until we could meet and talk it all out together. The date was fixed for 15 May, only ten days to go. It was for me to decide whether I wanted to fight and win and be married to Edward for ever, or divorce him and be free of him. As Philip put it: 'Pretend that you are in a taxi. The flag is up and I am the driver. You tell me where you want to go and I will put down the flag and get you there.' He, like my gentle lawyer Eugene Goodwille in New York, said: 'You are young and lovely. Don't dedicate your life to a hopeless future.' I thought and thought about it, and found it harder and harder to make up my mind, for it is my nature to forgive anything or anyone if I believe that they want to try again, and are sincere and really care. What a mug one is to always come back for more!

Thank God for Philip with his calm, wise counsel. The nearer the day to divorce I got, the more undone I became, for I could not get the feel of it or believe in any of it. None of it seemed real, just theory.

A few days before the hearing I got an anonymous telephone call from a strange man who said that he was speaking for Edward, who was not allowed to ring me. He said that whatever I did, I must not let the divorce go through as the evidence was a frame-up and Edward was helpless. This might have been a hoax.

Then the following day at five o'clock in the afternoon there was a light tap on my door. I thought that it was the maid, and when I opened it there was Edward, my husband! He took me in his arms, held me so close I could hardly breathe, and told me that he had slipped into the Dorchester by the side door in Park Lane and up the back lift unnoticed to avoid 'collusion'. Then we sat close together and he repeated all that the strange man had told me on the telephone the day before. Once the divorce was through there had to be six months' wait before it became absolute, and he could marry Jo. He wanted to marry me again! During that time he hoped that he could escape and come back to me.

In his distress he implored me to go on with the proceedings one minute and implored me not to the next. We both went to pieces, cried like children, and he left as suddenly as he had appeared. The loneliness and pain of it all was too much, so I told Philip, who listened with patience. But it was still up to me.

Two days later Philip drove me to the High Court of Justice. I was as cold as ice and my heart was stone. We had to wait a while until the previous case was over. Philip took me into the tea-room to give me a cup of tea. Then it happened! In the hall on our way, there was Edward with his lawyer, and as we passed he rushed over to me, nearly weeping with sadness, saying: 'Don't do it. Don't do it. You are the only one I love.' How much can one bear? Philip took my arm and steered me away into the tea-room and tried to help me pull myself together. The bell rang and made me jump out of my seat. Our case was next and I was shaking with nerves. How I got into the courtroom I will never know, for as soon as we entered, Philip went into one bench and I was put into another. I looked from where I sat waiting to go into the witness box and saw the terrible answer I had been waiting for!

Behind Edward stood six witnesses to testify against me if I did not divorce him!

My name was called and I was led up to the witness box. The judge was telling me to swear 'the truth, the whole truth, and nothing but the truth' and in five minutes, in a steady, clear voice, to my amazement, I had divorced Edward, my adorable husband for desertion, and it was over and I died inside. Philip never said 'Well done' or anything. He just stayed around, picked up the pieces and tried to help me to put them together again. Never was I more grateful for such a good friend. Without him I would have collapsed in the witness box. So it was done, and I was completely alone and in a state of shock.

Helen and Uncle Edgar D'Abernon took me down to Stoke

D'Abernon and made me feel that I still belonged to them, bless them. That meant such a lot to me; when Maudie, whom I was sure would drop me, because royals usually don't accept a divorcée, rang me and asked me to come and stay with her at Updown House in Sunningdale, I couldn't get over such warmth and kindness. My spirits rose with new hope. I was the innocent party, so I was acceptable in all circles, the Royal Enclosure at Ascot and at all Court functions. I received a letter from the Lord Chamberlain telling me this, and that I would be known in future as 'Rafaelle, Duchess of Leinster'.

During those six months of probation, Edward tried again to see me, but the wound had begun to heal and I could bear no more. I still saw that hideous line-up of witnesses in court, and thought he jolly well deserved to lose me. That court-scene was the fatal blow that set me free, and I too wanted to escape right away.

I clung to Philip, the D'Abs and dear little Maudie, who so bravely stood by me and up for me wherever her small voice could be heard, for there was real affection there, and I treasured it. Poor little soul, she was lonely and needed a friend from the world outside her own. Charles had to be in Scotland at Kinnaird, and she was alone much of the time at Updown— a house in a garden surrounded by rhododendrons—except for Jamie when he was home from school, and her sister, Princess Alexandra, the Princess Arthur of Connaught, who had a house nearby. There was also Princess Patricia, who was known affectionately as 'Princess Pat' by her regiment, of which she was Colonel-in-Chief.

This was the setting and world of royal talk that Jamie was brought up in. He would succeed to his mother's rank of Fife and become the Duke of Fife. Princess Arthur also had a son, the Earl of Macduff, and how fate was to strike and ring the changes. Time alone told that sad tale.

I spent many Septembers at Kinnaird Castle with Charles and Maudie and Jamie, after Charles succeeded to the earldom and they became the Earl and Countess of Southesk. Jamie was no longer Master of Carnegie, but Lord Carnegie, and there were high hopes that one day he would marry royalty.

How often have I sat in the gardens at Kinnaird and walked with Maudie, just a little way before she would have to sit down to get her breath, for she had asthma, and the Scottish climate did not suit her. The climb up the stairs inside the castle to her apartment was long and steep, and she had a chair put on each landing so that she could sit down and rest. Yet, she was so young at heart, and loved to dance reels when there were parties in the castle or at Braemar Gathering or Aboyne. But she found it too much for her, so I often took her place to dance opposite her partner. How I adored the reels and life in Scotland; I preferred it to England every time.

Many nights I have slept in the room opposite hers in Sunningdale, with both our doors open at her request, in case she needed help. She had what she called 'sleepers' in the drawer of her bedside table, and when she got into bed she would take one and ask me to sit on her bed until she felt she was 'going off'. When I saw her getting drowsy, I would tiptoe across the hall to my room, where I slept little, for I kept listening for her to call. I was afraid I would not hear her, for her voice, as I have said, was small and gentle. But all I heard was the big white owl in the wood that lay between the houses of the two Princesses, Patsy and Maudie.

Diana Smiley, now Lady St Aldwyn, was with her the weekend she had her fatal attack of asthma. Diana drove up with her in the ambulance when she was taken to her sister's nursing home, the Princess Arthur Nursing Home. Charles was sent for, and came at once. He had to take the day train having missed the night train from Aberdeen, and nearly missed that! By the time he got to the nursing home with Jamie, Maudie was still alive, but very weak indeed. A few days later she began slipping away.

Charles was in such a state of nerves that he kept running back and forth from the nursing home to me at the Dorchester. I had to speak at a Foyle's Luncheon at the Dorchester, and right in the middle of my speech the Master of Ceremonies came up behind my chair and put a note in front of me. It said that there was an urgent royal call on the telephone. I had a pretty good idea what it was, so I quickly ended my speech, to the relief of all I am sure, and went to the call box in the hall. There was Charles ringing from the nursing home, overcome with grief. Maudie was sinking and could I come quickly.

Less than half an hour later, Charles and Jamie were with me in my room on the top floor, their hearts broken. Charles was all in a heap of sorrow and shock, so it fell to me or Bob Maurice to tell the palace! To arrange a funeral was more than Charles could cope with in his distress, so in stepped Bob Maurice, an admirer of Maudie's, who took over and managed everything from that day onward. Poor little Jamie and Charles could do nothing except cling to each other. Bob was efficient, took on the responsibility and was now in his glory. Maudie, to everyone's surprise, had asked to be cremated. So up to Golders Green we went on a cold grey day, and sat side by side in that silent, chill, small chapel where a princess lay in her coffin. There weren't many people present —mainly Charles' family, representatives of the royal family, Diana Smiley, a few close friends and myself, sitting just behind Jamie and Charles. It was the first time I had been to a cremation, and I will never forget the terrible moment when the coffin started to move, oh so slowly, to and through the little door that slid open to receive it. I wanted to cry out 'Stop', but Charles broke down and Jamie too, so I reached forward and put my hand on Charles' shoulder, for he was shaking with grief. All that remained was a small pile of ashes and a handful of mourners.

Charles and Jamie came back with me to the Dorchester. I gave them tea, and we sat together in sadness. Charles had to get back to Kinnaird and he took Jamie with him. They made me promise to follow, which I did in a short time. I did not go up for the pathetic burial service in the family cemetery. That was entirely for father and son. Just a small urn in Scottish ground. Then I got a call from Charles asking me to write an obituary of Maudie for the newspapers! Never had I written such a thing, but I was so touched by the request that of course I agreed. Fancy it falling to me, an outsider, to do! Again it had to be sent to the king and approved. I had loved Maudie very much, so it was not at all difficult to write it.

Before I went up to Kinnaird, there was much to be done about the house in Sunningdale and Maudie's private papers and possessions. Bob was in charge of her affairs, but this pitiful task of sorting out some of Maudie's secrets was left to me. However, Charles was so lonely ringing me up night after night to come north, that I climbed into the Scotsman at King's Cross and jiggled and rattled my way through the night to Aberdeen, where I arrived at seven o'clock in the morning when it was still quite dark.

The car met me and drove me to the castle. Charles was not around. However, it was like home to me, the lean halls of Kinnaird, and I was taken to the same room I always had next to Maudie's; it was from here that she and I had heard the ghost walk at midnight. Charles appeared in time for breakfast, biting his moustache like mad, as was his habit when he was very upset, which was most of the time. We walked round and round the big dining-room with its tall windows looking on to the park and all the highland cattle 'moofs', as Maudie called them, each carrying our bowl of porridge. It's an old Scottish custom to stand or walk when you eat porridge—don't ask me why—so I'd got the hang of it after so many years of visits there.

As I have told you, Charles was inclined to be restless, critical and cautious, but there was a great sweetness and kindness in him, as I was about to find out. Almost as soon as I arrived I fell ill, and could not leave my bed for several days. He had even been called ungenerous, but I found him tender, generous and extremely patient and kind. He telephoned London to my doctor and took great care of me. I wanted to go back to London, as I felt I was a nuisance, but he persuaded me to stay for three weeks.

When he put me on the night train to London he could not bear to see me go and wanted me to get out and come back to Kinnaird.

How lonely people are. Double or single, rich or poor, it's an illness that we all suffer some time in life. I felt that I should leave him for two reasons: firstly gossip, and, secondly, if he really wanted me for keeps he would tell me so in time. Strangely enough, Maudie had asked me on two occasions if I would marry Charles and bring up Jamie should she die. Of course I laughed it off at the time, but I realized now that it was no laughing matter, then or at any time. She had had some premonition that she would not live long and really wanted me to promise her that I would take her place. Even her sister, Princess Arthur, sent for me and told me so!

In the spring, Charles took me to Updown to help him deal with the contents of the house, which were to be sold. Meanwhile I got to work on Maudie's private papers. There is only one thing more painful than sorting out one's own papers and letters, and that is to have to pry into another's secret heart. It took me nearly three months, and I have promised myself that I will not leave such a distressing task for anyone when I am no more. It is indeed a labour of love, and tears you apart, searching among intimate hopes, dreams and disappointments.

There was to be a sale and all the furniture was ticketed. Some would go to Jamie and Charles, the rest would be sold at auction. Then Queen Mary wanted to come down to see everything before the sale. Charles wanted me there when she came.

I had always heard that whenever Queen Mary came to your home, if she admired any object, picture, or little piece, the thing to do was to say how honoured you were, and present it to her, no matter how great the value or how much you treasured it. Consequently, I believe Marlborough House was cluttered with gifts. I knew that when she came to Updown she would have a field day. She had already told Charles that she wanted to buy the little glass-fronted Sheraton cabinet in the drawing-room before the sale, and asked him to put her ticket on it. Charles didn't want to part with it, nor did he want to lose favour with the Queen, so I told him to present it to her and make her happy.

When the royal car arrived at the door, Charles and Jamie

were there to receive Queen Mary and the Princess Royal. I was in the drawing-room, standing in front of the coveted cabinet, as Charles was still in six minds about parting with it. Charles presented me to Her Majesty as 'Rafaelle', so she hadn't a clue who I was, unless her sharp eye remembered me from the Palace. I doubt it, for she was looking for the little cabinet, and I was trying to hide it and make two sweeping curtsies at the same time!

I was immediately won by Princess Mary, for she had the most beautiful speaking voice and quiet manner. She was shy and gentle, which endeared her to me at once. The Queen was something quite else: that wonderful perch hat and long straight greyish dress with two deep pockets low down in the front! It was a dress that only she could wear and still look like a queen in it.

Jamie stood in the shadows, saying nothing at all, and Charles said even less. Oh dear, dear, what a great help they were! The Queen wandered about, looking at things, and finally got the other side of me and spotted the cabinet. She had a pretty good idea I was hiding it, for she looked straight at me and her eyes were full of mischief. That's done it, I thought, as she began to admire it. 'This is the cabinet I like so much, isn't it, Charles? The one I spoke to you about. Isn't it pretty, and such a perfect size.' She looked hopefully at Charles. Not a word from Charles, except a hesitant 'Yes'. I remembered all the things in Maudie's room that had been laid out on the bed for inspection, handbags, fans, hats, gloves, furs and so on. This is the moment, I thought, to get them upstairs. So I told her about them. Like a child, her face lit up and she was away and up the stairs in a flash. Princess Mary went with her, but she soon reappeared, leaving her mother alone with the loot—for loot it was to her.

When the Queen came back downstairs twenty minutes later, she was a sight to behold. Her arms were full of most of the things I had laid on the bed! Fans, artificial flowers, brooches, pieces of lace, handbags and a hat. Why a hat? It certainly wasn't a perch! From the two low-down pockets of her dress were pieces of beading, more lace, various trinkets, pieces of

ribbon, and even string spilling out on to the floor. Bless her—
this adorable woman who was as human as she was a queen.
Her haul had delighted her. Now for the cabinet!

When she and Princess Mary were upstairs, I told Charles
that this was the moment to give it to her, as he hadn't any
choice anyway. So finally he offered it to her, and that was
the end of a perfect day. I found a piece of cellophane and
wrapped her jumble in it, gave it to her, swept another curtsy,
and they were gone; so was the cabinet!

Chapter 11

I thought that I would be lost and lonely, all alone in England with no husband, no family, not even in-laws, but this was not the case. I had more friends, beaux and fun than I had had for years. Philip became a good friend, so was Charles, and there were several new additions. How right I had been to come back and get free.

Now I must find a flat and put down roots on my own. I had seen the flat I wanted at 15 Grosvenor Square, just before war was declared. It had style and service; indeed it was unique so I went to have a look. I got only as far as the door, because the whole building had been commandeered by the American Navy, and every flat had been turned into offices for the personnel. The building belonged to a rich little Jewish gentleman from Czechoslovakia, who owned several blocks of flats in Grosvenor Square and Portland Place. He had shown me the flat at No. 15 before the war, so when he heard that I was back in London he wasted no time in ringing me and asking if he could come to see me to offer me the same flat again. Round to the Dorchester he came and drove me to Grosvenor Square to show it to me. I was just as taken with it as before, even though it was cut up into portable cubicles, as was every flat in the building, for the Americans.

As it still pleased me, I took it on long lease from the day the Americans left. I was delighted, and he said the rent was £350 a year, all in. Meanwhile, I stayed on in my big room at the Dorchester until my decree was absolute and the coast was clear.

Philip's hobby was doing up flats and houses. In fact, as soon as he finished one place he would move to another and start all over again. I liked his enthusiasm and taste, and learned such a lot from him. When it came time to do up my nest he would surely be the man to have around. Three months after I had settled on the pretty panelled flat, Mr C. rang me and told me that Sir Harold and Lady Zia Wernher had taken the big flat on the front and insisted on having my flat for their servants' quarters! Naturally I was very upset, but Mr C. assured me that the flat above mine was exactly the same and I could have that. I asked if I could go and see it, and he told me that I couldn't until the Americans had gone, which would be quite soon. He said: 'Won't you take my word for it that it is precisely the same flat only a floor higher? It is identical, I promise you, so don't worry.' The tiny bell began to tinkle in the back of my mind, as it always does when the note is not true, when I am talked into anything, or try to talk myself into something I haven't got the feel of. I had no reason not to believe him. Trust me to walk right into the trap.

I had the feeling that I was being had, so I went round to No. 15 with an air force officer called Dickinson to see for myself. As he was in uniform we were allowed into the building, and I took him first to show him the flat I had wanted and lost. We then went up to the one above that Mr C. had promised me was identical. There wasn't any flat at all! For three months I had been living in a dream, if with reservations. Mr C. had used me as bait, and when two other duchesses took flats there, I had served my purpose. I went to see him and let him have it. I was on the receiving end and he knew it, because I wanted service, and there was no other place like it in London.

There was still rationing and keeping house was something to avoid if possible. Mr C. then showed me another small flat at the back of the building, with nothing to recommend it, and then had a bright idea. Up we went to the sixth floor, which is at the top, and immediately I saw its possibilities. The servants' quarters and kitchen belonging to the big front flat could be cut off and made into a flat for me. The front flat had not been let as yet, so if I was quick I could have it, for less than the one I had lost. It would take months to get a permit to alter and build, but Mr C. feeling guilty, said that he would give me the workmen and *carte blanche* if I could tell them what to do, and if it could be done in a week-end without a licence.

It had five windows, a familiar view of St Paul's, a bathroom, and considerable space. Mr C. knew that he had treated me badly, and after all, three duchesses in the building are better than two! I said I would take it if my solicitor could see it first.

Something to build was to Philip like a carrot to a donkey, so he was round there in no time at all. Yes, he could see what needed doing and advised me to grab it. Needless to say, Mr C. raised the rent £100 when he saw that he had me hooked, but it was that or nothing, for flats in London after the war just didn't exist, and he knew it.

I had to take it, and we built it in a week-end. My solicitor got me a seven, fourteen, twenty-one years' lease, that has more than paid off.

I had always heard that a woman alone was taken advantage of, and the more unprotected she was the more she was prey. Well, I couldn't have been more unprotected. Mother had always pulled my chestnuts out of the fire. I had lived on the end of string, on her money, and there was always a Man Friday to fetch and carry and be the buffer. Mr C. was my first bad experience, but certainly not my last. With Philip as my friend and hero, I had someone to turn to, I was more than grateful and indebted to him for all his help. When I moved into my 'tree top', I needed his wise counsel more than ever. But for the first time in my life I began to live a little and to learn to walk alone.

The decree was made absolute, and Edward married the former Gaiety Girl in February. They went to the South of France, where she took a villa which she ran as a paying guest house. The adoring Scot came back from the prisoner of war camp and married Olga, a Russian who had now taken his fancy. My beloved little Maudie had died, and the familiar way of life was no more.

I had to begin all over again. However, I did have youth, looks, rank and know-how, and a sense of humour and fun, the gift of living on sixpence with style, and wearing my clothes with an air far beyond their cost. So why not have my cake and eat it? I'd have a go and learn the hard way, and like it. I wanted no more of the possessive, obsessive web of doom spun by my mother. I wanted to grow up and be as others. Was it too late when I had been a puppet for over forty years and only just found it out? Time would tell.

I was sorry to leave the Dorchester, where I had enjoyed such care and kindness. I had known the staff there for so many years. The tall, smiling doorman in the tall, cockaded hat, the porters, and the lift man who had seen my brother-in-law, Desmond FitzGerald, killed by a bomb in the war, and carried him to the field hospital. Mr Ronus, a quiet, able young Swiss was the new manager, and his little boy used to ride in on his tricycle every morning with the waiter who brought my break-fast. These were my friends, and I missed them. But to have one's own corner was an excitement and a challenge, for I had never set up house before by myself. Indeed, I was the first tenant in No. 15 since the war.

I had it painted *eau-de-Nil* throughout, which sounds very grand, for it was really tiny. I had two auction sales at Harrods of the furniture I had stored with them. It was a great success, as at that time the demand for furniture was far greater than the supply. It did a lot for me psychologically, as I had nothing left to lean against, except the few pieces of value which I kept for my 'tree top', and I either added or replaced treasures as time went on. I didn't know anything about antiques, but I learned by observing, and walking many miles seeking and finding. I became completely fascinated, and having a natural eye for beauty and quality, and not a penny to lose, I seldom went wrong. Each treasure I found was an achievement. Every weekend I would go to the markets, and search and search, or wander about old streets unfrequented by all but dealers, and find things. The owners of the barrows and shops were helpful and kind, for they saw at once that I knew nothing at all. They would say: 'Take it home and try it, love, and if you don't like it, bring it back.' They too became my friends, and in their generous way taught me all I know. It may not be much, but it's a lot more than I knew when I started, and has paid off in both pleasure and pounds. For antiques are now worth double the price of a few years ago. The only thing is that it becomes an illness, and you can't stop. Happily, my nest is so small that there isn't room for more than me.

Then one day I found the jack-pot! The sort of *bonne chance* you dream about that never happens. This time it happened to me! I was walking along James Street, and passed a junky antique shop with a stall out on the street. I had been in it before several times, but I had not found anything very exciting. However, always tempted, I went in again, and there on a shelf behind some odd bits and pieces, I noticed a little bronze lady. I reached up and took her down and thought how lovely she was. I know little or nothing about bronzes, except what Marcus Cheke, a former ambassador to the Vatican, taught me. He was a collector and connoisseur, and gave me a small bronze head which I treasure. I felt the quality and looked to see if she was signed. She was! Somehow I felt I had really found something. So at the stall-owner's suggestion, I brought her back in my string bag. To cut a long story short, I paid eight guineas for her and she is still with me and very happy. I nearly lost her to Mallets, who wanted to sell her for £100. I then ran all the way with her to Sothebys where I was told that she would fetch £200 in a sale, or more, but to hang on to her as she would go up and up in value with the years. Needless to say, she continues to delight me—Psyche is her name—and to grow in value in more ways than currency. She is my small miracle and reminds me every day that to seek is to find.

The only old friends that I had in London were Sir Howard and Lady Kerr. He was Comptroller to the Duke of Gloucester, and a merry soul was he! Christina, his wife, adored him and her two huge spaniels. They had three sons who came and went. I loved How and Christina, and needed their welcome hearth, where I was truly happy and grateful. Stoke D'Abernon had been taken over as a diplomatic college during the war, and Helen was living in the stable. I wrote to her and she said that she would like to see me again when she felt able, and the sting of the divorce had passed. So the nearest thing I had to a family were the Kerrs.

Copsie, the head butler and I were the first to move into No. 15. He had been first footman with the Linlithgows and knew his work to perfection. So with him to rely upon I was proud to be a hostess and gave many dinners. Lord and Lady Wavell were at one and Alec Telfer-Smollet who asked all of us to stay with him at Cameron when Lord Wavell was to receive the Freedom of Perth.

It was the greatest fun in Alec's house on the banks of Loch Lomond. Archie Wavell was there to go to Perth, as Commanding Officer of the Black Watch Highland Regiment, to receive the Freedom of the City. Archie was a shy, gentle, quiet man with one good eye and one quite blind. On our way to the function I sat between Queenie and Archie in the back seat of their car. I liked them a lot, especially Archie, and we got on well together. He was in full-dress Black Watch tartan for the occasion and wearing a bonnet. Now Archie wanted to wear his glengarry, which was just behind me above the seat. His good eye kept glancing covertly back at it, but Queenie said 'No'! Poor sweetie, I thought, how he wants that cap. So when her ladyship was looking out of her side window, I reached back and got it and slipped it to him. He smiled like a child, and quickly took it and pushed it down beside him on the far side of the seat. When we arrived with full fanfare at the reviewing stand, off went the tammy and on went the glengarry. And when he took the salute, he was a man, in full command of his world.

I married first an Englishman, then an Irishman, but never a Scot, though I came mighty close on three occasions: one was a Highlander who eyed me from afar, then near. He looked well in his Highland dress when I met him at Oban, but not so glamorous when he came to call in London. Never will I forget his walking up and down, up and down, for one solid hour, trying to get the words out.

'Rafaelle dear, could you, well, what I mean is, would you,' and so on into the night.

Twice I was proposed to by proxy, once by Princess Arthur

of Connaught for her brother-in-law, and again by the Marchioness of Londonderry for her son. Neither asked me herself.

A grand Dame, known as Circe, was a remarkable woman. She was a great hostess and a social and political figure. Her balls at Londonderry House were scenes of great splendour before the war, and a meeting place for world figures and the élite of Europe. She wore a tattooed snake twining up one leg, a live screaming macaw on her shoulder, who bit you if you came too near, and a diamond tiara at functions that would knock your eye out. This imposing, powerful, adorable woman took me under her wing. I was thrilled, especially when she called me her kinswoman, which I was only by marriage. She wanted me in the family, and set out to try to make me her daughter-in-law, which touched me deeply.

Her son was her delight and worry. She had tried everything to help him, then me! She couldn't have chosen anyone less able to cope than myself. But when Circe made up her mind, that was it. She had made up her mind that I was the answer to his problem, and all her own! One day when she drove me back from Londonderry House, she said, 'It really isn't fair is it, to offer you up to another problem of the nobility, but I know that you are the one for my son, and I would be so proud to have you for my daughter-in-law.' I was both impressed and frightened, and very fond of her. So when she wrote me several letters from Ireland asking me to charm her son, and sent me postcards to remind me of him, I had little choice! In one of her letters she asked me to come to stay. I flew over to Nuts Corner, the airport also for Glenveagh, where I often stayed. This was a stately home indeed and a fair sight as I came up the long drive to be met by a brilliant peacock with his tail like a tremendous fan waving as he bowed to me several times.

It was here that I first encountered the macaw perched on my hostess' shoulder, and yet another snake. Only this one was real. Her daughter had several tanks and cages like a small zoo in her room, full of snakes, mice, monkeys, fish, and one furry little chap that swung by his tail, and looked at you with sad button eyes. The first night I was there, her favourite snake had disappeared and was last seen slithering towards my door! Well I prefer a snake to a spider, but I could have done very well without either. While I was dressing for dinner, I heard a little noise that sounded like something trying to crawl in. I tiptoed to the door from where the muffled sound was coming, and swung it wide in case whatever it was was in a hurry. There on his knees, was a fellow guest, looking for the snake of course!

When Circe returned to London, she was pleased and excited with a plan she had dreamed up of taking me to her son's house, Wynward Park, in Durham for Christmas. He must propose to me in the same drawing-room that her husband proposed to her. There was no turning back, even if he or I wanted to. I didn't want to. I was caught up in her excitement, and rather looking forward to what would happen. I was quite sure that her son hadn't a clue, and that we would both feel like the pandas, Chi-Chi and An-An. But why not let dear Circe have her little fun?

Before our arranged Durham romance, R. asked me to dine alone with him at his house in Park Street. Here it comes, I I thought! Heavens, I was nervous, for I hadn't expected this! Shaking in very pretty satin slippers, I went to dine. R. was quite himself—indeed I had never seen him otherwise. He was polite and cold, and told me that he had tickets for the theatre, therefore we had better have dinner at once. During dinner I took the prize.

We had paté as a first course. The butler passed a silver sauce boat with a spoon in it. Nothing very unusual about this, but the sauce was clear. I started putting it on my plate, when I noticed a terrible silence. R. said, 'It's hot water.' 'I know, said I, 'I like it that way.' What could you do with such a chump from Brooklyn, who went right on putting hot water all over the plate? The spoon, as everyone else would know, was in the hot water to keep it hot, so that it would slice the paté more easily without sticking.

Well, I saw Durham go out of the window, and I nearly

went out of it myself. We got through dinner, we got through the play—which R. hated and I neither saw nor heard—and we got through the courtship that never was, and not many weeks later, R. died from the water of life.

Poor Circe! She never got over losing her son, and it wasn't very long before she followed him. Never will I forget her standing once more at the top of the stairs receiving the guests at her grand-daughter's débutante ball. It made one want to weep, for the dread disease was stronger than she. I watched her sway and hold on to her daughter, for support. She had become very frail and her jewels seemed too heavy; alas, the magnificient tiara had already slipped. She hung on and received as many guests as she could, then she reached out for me to support her other side, still smiling and gallant, until she slumped into a chair and looked like a cherished rag doll.

Why is it that none of the men who asked to marry me, ever had any money? Except one—a million-dollar American. His wooing was something! He used to tell me how he would 'tap on my bedroom door and enter in the most alluring state of cleanliness and cologne to consummate the marriage'. What a ghastly thought!

Another Scot who smiled on me—only he never smiled—came from a well-known family and was mightily rich. Needless to say, he did not ask for my hand but he did ask me to stay, not at his place in the North, but at an imposing house he had taken in the South for pheasant shooting. There were quite a few guests for the week-end and these included a Lord-in-Waiting, an Ambassador and his pretty young wife, and a lady-in-waiting for me.

Here I was to meet my Waterloo—comparable to my experience at the Palace when Lady R. called me out of the procession. I thought I had learned about Englishwomen from her, but I hadn't learned a thing.

The first night, after dinner, when the ladies left the men to their port, brandy and talk, there was considerable grumbling about the lateness of the evenings, for we had to wait for our host and the rest of the men to join us and make more talk before we could go to bed. A hostess usually takes her ladies away either before or after coffee, depending where it is to be served. In about twenty minutes or so, the men follow, and the hour is not late, but a bachelor is inclined to indulge himself, and man-talk after the women have gone is to his liking. Affairs of state and the world are settled, and with my host, an hour would easily pass before the ladies were joined by the gentlemen. It was exhausting, and we longed to tell our host, but I am sure that this had always been the habit in his house.

Not having been there before, I didn't know the form, but I accepted it, even though I too was wilting, so I did what I was asked, by a guest, to get the ladies away.

'Our host is so taken with you, duchess. We will suggest that you play hostess to him tomorrow night when there will be more people coming to dine, then you can get us away. He will be delighted to see you at the head of his table and, incidentally, he thinks you quite beautiful . . . he told me so.'

Woe is me, I fell for it and the chance to feel like one of the girls, always feeling out of my depth.

Wouldn't you think that wide-eyed Rafaelle would have learned her Ps and Qs by now? No not this tail-wagging, eager-to-please gauche American! We were twenty-four at dinner. Everyone had been so friendly to me all day that I was in my foolish element. It was gay and glamorous and I was so proud to sit opposite my host at the long table.

Acting as hostess, the placement was accordingly. When the moment came for me (I thought) to make the move, I caught the eye of the principal guest. I nodded to her and rose . . . God help me I rose . . . and a roar came from the opposite end of the table.

'WHAT is happening?'

I knew then what I had done . . . and what had been done to me. We were all standing . . . my host with a face of granite said 'Of course', and I wanted to rush from the room, and rush from the house, and run all the way to London. This was the gaffe of all gaffes. In the morning, after a sleepless night, I left

. . . my host was not there to see me off, and I was never asked again.

When I was made Overseas Chairman of the Returned British Prisoners of War Association, a young Polish prisoner used to follow me about like a shadow. Then there was the very tall too-young man who found me in the gardens at Henry McIlhenny's Castle on the loch in Donegal. That was disaster, caused by the need for human warmth, even though we did not speak the same language in any sense of the word. Barbara Cartland, the novelist, once told me: 'Darling if you are looking for heart, you will only find it in the ordinary people.' How right she was, but how do you communicate?

I enjoyed seven happy visits, for seven happy years at Glenveagh Castle, until this youth smiled upon me. I always had the same room in the tower that looked up the loch, from which, on stormy nights, the wind bowled down the loch to my window in the tower, landing with a mighty wallop that nearly blew me out of the giant four-poster bed. The only thing that did drive me out—and on three occasions—was when the wind blew a bat into my bed! Its whirring wings and terrified squeaks sent me flying out into the candlelit hall with the eiderdown over my head. Poor Henry was wakened each time by my shenanigans; he came out of his room to see what was going on, and tore back into it again like crazy when the bat followed me into the light, then him back into his room!

Glenveagh is a divine place to stay. You couldn't have a more charming host. His sense of things beautiful and comfortable made you want to stay forever.

Young Princess Elizabeth now became Queen on the death of her father. Naturally, with this young couple at the Palace, I thought that my days were numbered for grand occasions. It was so soon after the war and invitations to functions were few . . . everyone's jewels were in the vaults. But the Queen must be crowned, and the date of the third coronation in England during my lifetime, was proclaimed.

Only reigning peers and peeresses could be summoned to the Abbey for this august ceremonial. They would come in their wonderful red velvet ermine-trimmed robes, carrying their coronets to place upon their heads when the royal crown was placed on Her Majesty's. Certainly no such glory as this was for me, for I was no longer a reigning peeress, and my duke had never been welcome. But Cinderella was born again, and to my amazement, it was me! How did I come to be asked? Well, not in my fine robes as a peeress of the realm, and not in a coach and four, but in a borrowed car, and my Prince Charming was a policeman on a motor bike! I went to represent the British POWs. My dress was gold gossamer, and there were diamonds in my hair. I went by myself, as usual, and saw the sight of any American girl's lifetime, and was a part of that historic, breathtaking scene. The chauffeur who was lent to me was a country lad, and had to sleep in the big entrance hall of the block of flats where I live, as we had to leave at six in the morning. Why I went to bed at all I don't know, because I was so excited I couldn't even shut my eyes. I kept saying: I must get up at four o'clock. Oh dear, will it ever get light? What time is it now, only two! and now, only three! Well this is hopeless, let's get up, surely it's nearly four. How dark and cold it is. How will I keep warm in the Abbey? Woollen knickers— I must, or I will freeze. They and my ermine cape should keep me warm. Fancy putting on my lovely golden dress and my tiara at four fifteen in the morning! Let's see what is going on outside. Heavens, what a lot of windows are blazing with lights! Good, that wakes me up from the sleep I never had. I must make some coffee and eat something, for I won't have a proper meal until nightfall. Thank goodness Tom the chef will have a package of sandwiches ready for me and the Buccleuchs who will also be going from here to the Abbey.

Would six o'clock ever come? We had to be in our seats in the Abbey before seven thirty that morning. My maid, Marden, had come to help me dress, for the pleasure it gave her to see and know someone who 'would be there'. I was tense and rather nervous as I went down in the lift, supposedly to pick up my lunch and strange chauffeur and be on my way. As I stood in the hall asking where my lunch was, I was told that the chef had overslept and there wasn't any lunch! Just at that moment, a motorcycle policeman came in at the front door looking for the owner of a car that had been parked outside. He meant to arrest the owner, for parking was not allowed anywhere in central London on this great day. Instead of getting on with his job, he caught sight of me, sparkling from head to foot, and he stopped still, staring at me. He saw my distress at having no lunch, and forgot everything that he had come to do. 'Madam,' he said, 'I don't know who you are, but I can't let such a beautiful lady as you go to the Abbey without anything to eat. I would be so pleased if you would accept my packet of sandwiches the wife made for me.'

He pulled a brown paper bag out of his pocket and put it in my long white gloved hand. What a kind and touching thing to do. I took the bag gladly and he took me out to the car. He saw at once that my country chauffeur did not know the proper route, and he mounted his motorcycle and said; 'Follow me!' He started us off, touched his cap, and was away. Well, so were we, the wrong way! The driver hardly knew London at all, so we had to help each other the best we could through streets lined twelve deep with tired, happy people who had spent the night on the pavements. Any little excitement cheered them— even me in my borrowed car and borrowed finery. How many wrong turnings could we take? Finally, one hour late, we battled our way to the entrance door.

I was taken to my seat in the second row right over the great west door. What a view! I couldn't have wished for better. My companions were diplomats and I was in happy company. I was relieved that there was a rail in front of our seats, because the Pakistani minister on my left kept falling asleep, and the only thing that kept him from falling on top of a Zulu chief in front of him was the cold brass rail that caught him as he toppled forward.

It was a tremendously long wait, and I gave up counting the minister's narrow misses. There was a charming diplomat's wife on my right who had a sense of humour and a box full of glucose tablets. I had fortunately taken lumps of sugar in my bag, so we fed each other these sustaining sweets, and I never felt tired or hungry during those long eight hours.

Only once I went out to powder my nose, and then ate a banana that was in the policeman's paper bag. I needed no more. It was a long wait, but there was so much to watch and see that the hours passed quickly, especially when the fanfare announced the approach of the Queen and the magnificent procession that preceded her began to move. But the thing that pleased me more than all else was the small army of women who went on to the blue carpet with carpet sweepers and swept the whole length of it in herringbone pattern, quickly, efficiently, and as one. They were in blue uniforms, and the sweepers were also as blue as the carpet. No ballet has given me more pleasure than they did. For this is my own private ballet. When each day is done, all must be in order before a new day is born. Out comes my sweeper—no matter the hour—to smooth the marks of restless feet and any trace of conflict, so that I can rise and shine on the morrow.

When the royal people came slowly onto this immaculate carpet, it was like a blue lawn. Another queen who stole the show was Queen Salote; of great height and dignity, she towered over all the others. The Queen Mother, in purple velvet robes, was a small but glorious figure, but one was so dizzy with the splendour and the music and singing that one could hardly take it all in. One thing that I was constantly aware of was that I had the best seat in the world, and had I been in my former rightful place, I would have missed all this.

I was privileged indeed, and when we all rose to shout 'God save the Queen', I thought that I would faint from emotion. I wanted to add, 'and God save the POWs!' Not only did I see them all go in, but I saw them all come out, all the way from the throne, the little Queen wearing the heavy jewelled Crown of State and even heavier mantle and carrying the orb and sceptre; the bells pealing, the crowds shouting, and the skies pouring with torrents of rain!

No one could leave the Abbey until the Queen and royal party were *en route* to the Palace. I saw this drive later on television, with Queen Salote in an open carriage waving and smiling all over her black face, just as though the sun was smiling too, while the heavens opened and soaked the world.

Finally we were allowed to leave. It was four thirty in the afternoon, and then came the long wait for the cars to be called. As we drove through the sodden streets, knee-deep in wet newspapers and wildly cheering rain-soaked people, I thought, this is England, and for these few hours in my life, I have been a part of it. It was worth all the years that had gone before and those that were to come.

Quite a lot followed in the years that were to come, up there in my tiny 'tree top'. Believe it or not, I received three more proposals of marriage. The third proposal was from . . . my husband! One fine day, indeed the only fine day of summer that year, the telephone rang at about five thirty in the afternoon and a familiar voice said, 'Hello, is that Rafaelle . . .?' 'Hello Imp,' said I, knowing his voice at once, to his surprise and delight.

'How did you know it was me?' he asked. 'I would know your voice anywhere, and at any time,' I said. 'Could I come and see you? I have missed you,' to which I told him he would be most welcome. Almost before I could hang up he was round. He must have rung from the call box across the road, to the head porter's horror, for he was announced as Mr FitzGerald, and spoken of as 'a person', as servants will when they do not approve, for they are not always discerning.

Bless my Imp's heart, there he was, looking like a wanderer, getting out of the lift with his arms open ready to enfold me. I must say I understood our pompous porter's reservations about his appearance, but this was the state that I had found him in when we first met. It always shocked me, but I knew that with a little scrub and polish wonders could happen, for his breeding was eloquent. Awkwardly he thrust a parcel into my hand It was a lovely Worcester china swallow!

When I think of the months and months that I had spent

hoping and dreaming of this moment! Why, God knows, after
the nightmare our marriage had been, but I can only think that
when one is deeply fond of someone in spite of everything, this
affection never dies. Also, as I have said, I prefer the devil I
know to the devil I don't know. Here then, was the second
chance that I thought would never come. I was very pleased,
but it was late, very late, and I had begun to learn to refuse
the pain of living. A form of self-denial, I suppose you could
call it, for I could not bear to have another little animal to hold
and cosset and lose, or another heart that would desert me.

My poor Imp! How sad and harassed he looked, and completely down and out, with a pathetic happiness at being with
me again. We held each other close, then he began to wander
about the flat, touching familiar objects and finding his way
back to yesterday. I wanted to cry as I watched him. Then he
saw his mother's miniature lying on a small table and went to it
as though she had spoken. His eyes filled with tears as he picked
it up and said: 'Could I take her with me for a little while?
I promise to return her.' 'She is your mother,' I said. I knew
that I would never see it again, but so what, she belongs to
him.

There was a childlike elation about him, as though he had
come home after a long and exhausting journey. Well, so he had
in a way, and I was touched and thankful that he had. But I
sensed danger.

He soon sat down, delighted with the little flat, and to see his
full length portrait hanging by the front door and began to tell
me about his unhappy life and some new schemes to buy back
his Life Interest and several new found backers. How many
times I had heard that one before! But what seemed to be
uppermost in his mind was his sorry state of matrimony. He
kept on asking me why I had let him go and why I had let him
marry 'that woman' as he called his third abandoned wife. You
knew what she was like and what she was up to and should
have prevented it!

Oh dear . . . where do you take it from here? He then
rammed his hands into his bulging pockets trying to find some

So Brief a Dream

snapshot he wanted to show me. 'Ah . . . here they are darling,' he said proudly as they spilled on to the floor, just as those dollar bills had spilled on to the steps of St Patrick's Cathedral in New York over twelve years ago. As usual I began picking them up, out of habit. He said that he had a rendezvous in Hyde Park in an hour's time with friends. Would I please come with him to meet them! I dodged this situation, but there were soon others and for his sake I tried to take some of them in my stride.

When he had bolted from Jo, he took shelter as Mr Fitz-Gerald in one guest house after another. Never keeping enough money for essentials, he had apparently managed to live on promises and romance. I did go with him to meet some of these people who he said had been kind to him but they were dynamite. The pitiful part of it all was that Edward saw them as angels of mercy, and wanted them to see and meet the one thing he was proud of, myself.

As the months passed, he became younger and happier, feeling that he could run in and out of Grosvenor Square. He lunched almost every day with me in the restaurant downstairs. As for the startled, gossiping tenants, we made their day! The newspapers soon had it in England and USA, and we were beginning to be the 'talk of the town'. A young admirer of mine was having a fit, as he had his calculating eye on security, and the Italian ambassador, Count Zoppi, was more than a little taken with my charms. The day he sent me a present from Harrods of all places, I took it back within the hour and exchanged it for the loveliest little brass inlaid mahogany chair. I thought, That will teach him—and it did!

While all this performance was going on, with suitors ringing bells and running up and down the lift and stairs, Edward decided to move in! Bless him, sitting there in the chair opposite me in my blue drawing-room, he asked me if I would please marry him again! How I loved him for it! It was the greatest compliment of my life, and the moral stigma of having been left was gone for ever. Feeling the pull at my heart, and knowing that the goblins would get us if we didn't watch out, I

G

169

thought it prudent to fly to New York, as I had been doing for the last two years at Christmas time, to be with my mother now that she was alone. If I wasn't careful, I, the ex-wife, would be sued by the present wife as co-respondent! And that would be the story of the year! I also thought it would give him time to get free, and for me to be quite sure that I was ready and able to walk right back into the lion's mouth again.

Edward saw me off at the airport, and said that he would be there to meet me on my return. Meantime, he would ask for a divorce. We sat in the VIP waiting-room for my flight to be called. He seemed unable to bear the parting and I was about to cancel my flight and stay with him. But just then the BOAC official came to take me to the plane, and somehow I blindly went and left this lonely, hapless man who was trying so hard not to cry.

It is so hard to do the right thing when it comes from the head and not the heart. I wanted to be wise and brave and sensible for both our sakes, but I wasn't making a very good job of it. It took me a long time to get my bearing thirty thousand feet up in the sky. Seven hours to be exact, and when I got to New York, I felt tired and older than God. Edward wrote me a few wistful notes asking me to come back. I hoped that he would say something about the divorce, but he didn't.

He sounded so lost and lonely. Then I heard from my stepson—Edward had taken an overdose and tried to end his life! My poor little Imp, even that hadn't worked. He was the eternal earth-bound spirit, born to suffer from his own mistakes and cause more harm to himself than he ever intentionally inflicted upon others.

It seemed that he had gone to Dr Carey, my doctor, to get some sleeping pills, on the pretext that he could not sleep because of the severe pain in his knee. It was his only way of getting the pills and, before he took them in some ghastly bed-sit off Bayswater Road, he wrote me a farewell letter, telling me of his love for me. He would, he said, by taking his own life, be able to leave me better off than he had ever been himself while he lived. Gerald wrote me long before his father had attempted suicide, imploring me not to marry him again, as he said I had had more than my share, and would only be putting my head back in the noose. What Edward's reasons were for this pathetic dramatic attempt to die, I do not fully know, but it took a toll of his resistance. It didn't work, and did no good to anyone, least of all himself.

When I flew to London three months later, there he was waiting for me with roses in his hand, but somehow I knew then that I could not make a life with him again. He would leave me a second time, as he could never stay anywhere or with anyone for long. However, he will always live in my heart, this adorable changeling, for even though his crown was tarnished and hollow, he taught me the quality of music, which is my happiness, and, I hope, the common touch. And I am sure that I am the only duchess of the realm who was ever asked by the same duke to marry him twice!

Back in my 'tree top' after another revealing look at mother, I still wore the feeling of guilt, and got a flat at 55 Park Lane for her to come to London for the summer. It had always been my dearest wish that mother should come to London for the summers with a reliable companion who would stay with her, and that I should go to New York for the winters. Mother loved England as I do, and it would be the perfect solution . . . and I could proudly show *her* off—for a change! I must have been living in Cuckoo Land to attempt such madness. I had her and the poor unsuspecting companion she had brought with her, met at Southampton by the car and chauffeur I frequently use myself.

I thought that the flat was fresh and pleasant, and I put flowers in it to welcome her. When she arrived, everything was wrong. She hated the flat and never saw the flowers. There was meal and room service in the building, and she would have none of it.

Let me tell you about her, this wilful, small rebel who was my mother and keeper of my soul. Wherever she went, people turned their heads to gaze and admire. Fragile, ancient and exquisite, with her lovely complexion and shining, abundant white hair swept up into a soft wave under her blue petal hat. She attracted all eyes and helping hands. What a tiny treasure to be proud of and to cherish, with her charm and winning ways.

Like a small Empress, she commanded attention, praise and pity, and above all, surrender, and got it. Brave as a lion, and cunning as a mouse, she dominated the scene and all who entered her realm. A mighty atom was she, yet so insecure, possessed by fear, afraid to live, afraid to die, dwelling in a world of panic, wilful woe, and utter waste. Isn't it strange that one so blessed by the gods should fight her way through ninety-three years of a good life without one major tragedy or illness, respecting no man, seeking and finding only the flaw?

Her mind darted to the right, darted to the left, refusing and rejecting fact, reason and sweetness, causing chaos, pain, pity, and fury, while she remained completely untouched herself, without any remorse. Such a pretty, lonely little *enfante terrible*.

Deaf to all sound, deaf to all joy, deaf to all friendship and laughter, deaf to the only one who cared. Yet God she heard. Isn't it strange? Well, there she was, my egocentric aggressive depresser, who kept me in style and comfort all my life, and at the age of nearly one hundred, lived on borrowed time and borrowed money which she gambled in the stock market on margin, and remained in the driver's seat at full speed ahead to God knows where!

Before she went back to New York, I wanted her to sit in a corner of the Albert Hall and see and hear a Promenade Concert conducted by Sir Malcolm Sargent. I had a reason—the best reason in all the world. Malcolm arranged for her to sit just inside the door at the top of the stairs nearest the stage with her companion of the day.

The big fight to get her there, and all the way there, in a car was enough to make one turn back. I was afraid of a scene when we arrived, and took her in the artists' entrance, and plonked her down where she was to sit and like it! The enormous crowd overwhelmed her, and she forgot herself and seemed to take an interest.

I knew she would hear little, but it was so important that she should see this fantastic sight of two thousand young promenaders standing on the floor below. They had stood outside through the night before to pack themselves into this seething mob, just to listen to music. She said that she wanted to leave as soon as Malcolm had appeared and conducted the overture. I was so nervous, not knowing what she might or might not do as I went round to the Maestro's box. I could see her from where I sat—such a pretty, tiny figure opposite me across the hall. I wanted to cry as I watched her when Malcolm made a bow to her and music began to fill the place. Mother seemed to be actually listening and hearing. I felt a great happiness and sadness, and somehow a light went out when she got up to go.

It has always been the same in the years that followed; when I sat there in Malcolm's box I could still see her sitting there, and feel my throat tighten with the tears of loving that I had stifled all my life. I must tell you that she was very cross at having to leave the Albert Hall that evening long ago, even though it had been the condition on which she would go at all. *Fait accompli* was the only way to tackle mother; allowing her no time to battle, but sometimes you dared not risk it.

She will haunt me in the Albert Hall as she haunts me in the little green gardens behind Farm Street Church. We used to meet there when she was in Park Lane, and I see her coming towards me in her blue flower hat, so elegant and small, and whenever I walk through Mount Street Gardens, the surge of loneliness fills my heart with an unrequited longing.

In almost all the other countless places where I stayed as a house guest, I was a very happy guest indeed. Only two visits came to a sudden end. The one at Eleuthera with Rosita Forbes had a short life and not a merry one.

It was a lovely island, with miles of beaches which I could have enjoyed had I not been kept to heel, but you did what Zita wanted. I got one swim, if you can call it that, working

my way through millions of crabs, lurking barracudas, and two
sleepless nights, not because of the rush of lizards on the ceiling
in my ground floor bedroom, but because of my disturbed
neighbours chasing a giant spider from dark till dawn, and a
mighty yelp from Zita! What had dropped on her? When I
asked her, I wished I hadn't. My fellow guests vanished the next
day. This was not a cosy, happy house. No one was natural and
I wanted to get out, like my friends next door. So I sent Lady
Beatty a telegram in Nassau, as she had warned me that I
would be sure to do, for she knew the form. The only snag was
that Arthur, Zita's sparring mate, got my telegram before it
was sent!

However, Dotty Beatty blew the whistle, as I hoped she
would, and I was soon away in the tiny aircraft that flew if and
when it could, weather permitting. When I got to Nassau, two
days after I had left, there was Dotty waving to me with her
short white gloved hand, calling out, 'Dr Livingstone, I
presume.' She didn't say 'I told you so'—she didn't have to!

My other hasty retreat was from Viscount Tredegar's house
in Surrey. That lasted only one night. When I met Evan at
Kinnaird in Scotland, where we were both staying with Charles
and Maudie Southesk, I found him highly intelligent, sensitive
and charming, and very easy to be with and to like. He was
Charles' cousin and, much later on, another member of
Charles' family who thought that I should become *châtelaine* of
Kinnaird.

Well, to get back to Evan. He used to drink a whole bottle of
brandy at night, and not turn a hair. I saw him do it at Kinnaird when on his way up to bed at night. He, Maudie and
Charles would stop at my room at the top of the stairs to gossip
some more. I hadn't a clue what it would be like, when he very
kindly asked me to stay with him in England.

When I arrived at tea-time by train, I was rather amused at
the group of young men who also got out at the same station
from the carriage behind mine. Four or five of them.

Were they too for Evan's? Yes . . . they all climbed into the
car that had been sent to meet me—so I knew what it would be

like and who my fellow guests were! They were different
nationalities and ages and all delighted to be where they were
. . . so the week-end would certainly not be dull!

The only other woman about the place was a weary housekeeper who had obviously been there a very long time. Evan
took me first to see his chapel on the top floor, before he showed
me to my room. I don't know which upset me more, for I
certainly was not ready for either. He was a devout Catholic,
indeed Papal Chamberlain, and spent hours in his small
sanctuary in prayer.

When I walked into the room I was to sleep in, I wanted
to run screaming into the night. It was lit only by candles, and
very dark, with the most sinister patterned wallpaper; over my
bed, a large portrait of Oscar Wilde. The colour of the drawn
curtains was red and instead of creating an atmosphere of
warmth it chilled me.

However I changed and went down to dinner. Dear eccen-
tric Evan was in a state of elation and was waiting to show me
his gift for Our Lady, a large beautiful diamond cross. The whole
situation seemed macabre when the others joined us, including
a young Scandinavian whom I had met in London, who must
have arrived late. We were given drinks and taken to see our
host's valuable collection of rare ivory figures. Rare to me
certainly, for I had never seen anything like them before! I was
embarrassed and frightened.

We eventually got through dinner and afterwards went into
the drawing-room. It was evident that the young men were
not as used to brandy as my host. Hysteria was in the room and
I couldn't bear another minute of it, whatever IT was!

I went in search of someone to see if I could get a train back
to London. Not a hope. No trains until the morning.

Well, it was another night to remember, and when daylight
came I didn't even wait for breakfast. I got a taxi, and to my
amazement, I found another guest also at the station. He looked
completely used up, and whipped out a big white pill saying:
'If I don't take this I will die!'

Thank God the train came, and I don't think he died, for a

year later I saw him in Grosvenor Square looking manly and
fit, and I decided that it was time that someone told me the
facts of life! It's not for me to sit in judgment of any man,
only please don't ask me to join in!

Chapter 12

As I have said, to keep the traffic one way, I went every winter to New York, usually by sea, in the wonderful *Queen Mary* and *Queen Elizabeth*—grande dames of the mighty ocean in war, in peace. In war, the great *Queen Mary* was a ghost ship and Werewolf of the sea to the Germans, as she went bearing her load of lives to and fro, scorning the deep-sea submarine pack. I sailed in them many times when they were palaces of elegance and comfort and enjoyed five days of fun in all weathers, always invited by the captain or commodore to sit by their side at their table among far more distinguished guests than I.

Commodore Ford with his great height and rolling gait was so right in size and presence for the flagship. I delighted in him and travelled with him many times. Also Captain Grattidge of the *Mary*, who told me to let him know if it got too rough when he stepped up the speed in the early hours, as I had told him that I had been on the floor once. It happened again, and I took him at his word and rang him on the bridge to say 'hello' from under my bed! How the *Mary* used to roll before she got her stabilizers, and how both *Queens* would leap and plunge, then settle and shake themselves like giant wet cats, then do it all over again and again. One had to hang on to ropes, the soup and the side of one's bed. Very tiring, but I loved it all and found it rather exciting.

When Cunard ships went on strike and I had to get back to England, Mr Franklin, owner of the United States Line, sent me off in the *United States*, a lovely ship as swift as an arrow, which could, I am sure, have made the crossing in three days if she could have been given full steam ahead. I don't know what kind of an entourage Mr Franklin had led his staff to expect, but when I was shown into my large and immaculate cabin, I found there a smiling coloured steward standing behind a long table covered with bottles, glasses and delicious things to eat! Did they expect me to arrive with a crown on my head, trailing twenty millionaires? What a let down: there was only me, myself, and I, with three suitcases, and—I don't drink!

Another captain I found charming was Captain Sorrell—so small in size, yet one never noticed, for he was so big as a man. His crew loved him and threatened to strike when protocol prevented him carrying the Queen Mother in the *Queen Elizabeth* to America. There were several other skippers whom I became fond of, for I was a frequent passenger; they are rather special men, these men of the sea, and were extremely kind to and careful of me. I take off my hat to each and all of them wherever they may be, who gave me their protection and hospitality. For when travelling alone, one is thankful for a base and welcome, and all my thanks to Cunard for their great care and courtesy over so many years.

Some think the captain's table is a bore. Not I, for there is always someone to make it sparkle, such as Lady C., who wrote a book on cats, and looked like a beautiful white Persian herself; she even made mewing sounds when she talked. And Lord A., who drank ten large glasses of orange juice at every meal. I know, I counted! Then there was Brenden Bracken, the Minister of Information in Mr Churchill's government. He looked like a great tawny teddy bear, and was worried about penicillin. He was allergic to it, and never let us forget it. And then there was England's most elegant foreign secretary, Sir Anthony Eden, and 'Pug' Ismay, Lord Ismay, who added lustre and fun to the parties I had, and interest and delight to all aboard the *Queen*. And a little lady, a most winning small dynamo of power and intellect, Helen Ogden Reid, owner of the *New York Herald Tribune*, who shone brightly in my life for many years. No, I never found any of it a bore. On an eight-day crossing in the *Queen Mary* from Southampton to New York, when the sea was so fierce that we were hove to for nearly a day, or crawled at snail's pace, hardly moving at all lest the terrific waves break the *Queen*'s back, Canadian-born Beverley Baxter MP, and the

American candidate for President and his wife were at our table. Even though we missed the captain, who was on the bridge most of the time, we were certainly never dull; not a bit, in fact, in such lively political company discussing world affairs. I listened a lot and learned a lot. What fascinated me most was the tea the Stassens drank from the beginning to end of every meal. They sat together; I could never understand why husbands and wives were always placed side by side at the captain's table, but they were. Surely they can do that at home!

I have said that I have never been bored at the captain's table, but sometimes one did have to work at it. The biggest challenge was my last journey in the *Queen Mary*. It really looked as if we were a load of characters, and I mean characters, but it became hilarious. Johnny Rogers MP was there and about to vanish at the sight of the table when we met. Then we took a good look at the table and each other and felt a mutual sense of fun that sent us spinning; we made the whole ship rock with laughter. Dear Johnny, sparkling humour, alive with feeling and perception. Even quiet Captain Divers was helpless with mirth, as were his Tiger and the stewards. This was hardly what to expect from the Navy and 'not done', but believe me it *was* done and the staff and passengers never stopped smiling.

Another character, an American, was travelling with his Mercedes Benz intending to 'do' all the countries of Europe in it. He wanted me to go along for the ride, but much as I like driving in a car, especially such a grand one, I thought better of it, and returned to my 'tree top', where he rang me from all the places he went. The last was Turkey. Perhaps he is still there, for I never saw or heard from him again.

All those years when I came to be with mother at Christmas, I would still feel the touch of sadness when I heard either *Queen* blow her farewell as she sailed back to England. I would feel left behind. I wonder why, for as I sit writing this in Madison Avenue the two royal sister ships are chained to American shores earning their keep like wild animals in a zoo. My own world has stopped, but I still want to weep as I hear the new

*QE*2 moving down the river, blowing one long, three short, with the same beautiful minor note.

I often flew out to New York in the fine BOAC jets to cut the time, for London is such fun the month before Christmas that I hated to leave. It breaks the continuity and takes weeks to pick up the threads and get into one's stride again when I return in the spring. It's such a mistake to be on the move every six months. You don't strike roots or become a permanent part of the scene.

I am a timid flier, flying comes next after thunderstorms and spiders! Even though I like it as a means of travel when all is well, each flight is my first and each landing is, I vow, my last. One flight in Pan Am nearly was my last. It was, as my compatriots say, a beaut! I think it was in 1967, when England was frozen solid to the ground for three days and so were all her planes.

I had packed away all my treasures in my flat and covered everything with dust sheets as I did each year, and was ready and waiting for the nice warm car I hire, with its kind and reliable young chauffeur to come to take me to the airport. Then I was rung and told that there would be an hour's delay in take-off. As the chauffeur was as punctual as usual, and I felt depressed sitting in front of one bar trying to keep warm, and very tired from the upheaval, my luggage was put in the car, and off we went. And what a shambles we found at the airport! Some aircraft coming in, some not coming in, and few, if any, taking off. People, people everywhere, standing, sitting, waiting, looking tired and worried, and the loud-speakers going full blast. Delays, delays, and then it came. Flight BOAC such-and-such to New York cancelled! Some of us were transferred to an incoming Pan Am flight on its way to London somewhere in the sky between France and England. After half an hour's wait, I heard it coming in and watched it skid and slide on the ice, and wondered if it could ever stop—to say nothing of how it would get going again! Most of the passengers were very uneasy—I know I was.

Finally we were told to board, if you can call it that, for it was almost strap-hanging. I sat near the back with a young mother and her small boy. She promptly told me that she was the wife of the pilot and the child was their son. I felt safer at once. Then we made a dash for a take-off and missed. Then we tried again, and everyone held their breath and by the grace of God we got off the frozen earth and soared up into the smiling sunny sky.

It took us eight hours to reach New York. Thank God there there was no blizzard to land in, but why didn't we land? We were told that we had to stack, as all the runways were full, so we stacked, and round and round we went until I was sure that the fuel would run out.

We seemed to have been up there over the airport for years, when we were told to come in. Down, down we slowly dropped with our mammoth load. The passengers perked up, and the pilot's son was watching for us to touch down.

'Wow!' he shouted, as a two-engine plane dived under us on our way down. Then, when he recovered from that too-near miss, he shouted that we were about to touch down, and both mother and child began bracing themselves for the bump which had to come with such a load, when there was a terrific roar, and all the lights went out. Everyone screamed, the loudest scream, 'This is it!' came from the pilot's wife! She dived down to the floor, as did the boy . . . I joined them! The roar of engines got louder and louder, and again, by the grace of the Almighty, we began to climb. We were in darkness, frozen with fear!

Again we stacked and, when we came in to land the second time, I don't think anyone even cared. When we touched the blessed earth and came to a halt, nobody moved. We couldn't; our legs wouldn't hold us—they were like jelly. Even the steward was unsteady, and his face was green. He took me off, and said that he would tell me at Customs what happened. I thought that he was being tactful and trying to comfort the passengers.

He did meet me at Customs, and what he told me was that a United Airlines aircraft had got on to our runway by mistake

So Brief a Dream

and had it not been for the great skill of the pilot and captain, it would have been the end. No one felt heroic, we were all too shaken, but I hope our pilot did, and that his wife and son are as proud of him as were all his passengers.

That year I noticed for the first time a deterioration in the depressing situation in the Gold Fish Bowl, which I called the large one-room flat with a balcony on the fifteenth floor at 750 Park Avenue. Here mother lived with one companion after another, acquired from newspaper advertisements and all mostly down-and-outs. They didn't last long; they had no privacy of their own, demands were made upon them which they were not trained to fill, together with constant fault finding.

My mother's interest and hobby was the stock market; she borrowed money from an ancient beau to gamble. For gamble it was, with little profit and mostly loss. She loved the excitement and being surrounded by men; this kept her young and pretty until the end. So no matter now bitter the pay off, I am grateful to the beau for the fun he gave her, even though the whole lot has to be paid back!

Her fear complex grew worse with time, and the increase of crime in city streets didn't help. Each night I went over to have supper with her. It became so embarrassing to get back two blocks to my hotel that I went less and less. She would ring the police and the hotel to post men on the corners to watch me dash from door to door in case I was raped! To go to dinner parties was shaming; she would ring to see if I got there, and then ring my hotel every hour on the hour to see if I had got back!

When I was with Tommy she didn't worry. Sometimes he and I went up to Schraffts to have dinner: not very smart, but less expensive than other restaurants. We sat at a table near the door, and on this evening I noticed a slight, very nice-looking young man with a whole brood of children waiting in the queue for a table. He looked so familiar that we felt we knew him. Of course, Bobby Kennedy with all nine children! His wife, Ethel, was not with him. She was awaiting their tenth! There he was,

182

alone with his young. Finally they were given a table near us and I have yet to see a happier group or better behaved children. This is saying a lot for American children, who play up their parents at home and become completely unmanageable in public. To see such a young father with nine well-mannered and well-behaved boys and girls in a public restaurant, unaware of all observers, told me something. Here was a natural, united, devoted family, where there was love and respect for a man who had indeed the common touch.

Each winter I stayed longer, seeing how dreadful things were, and went back to London only to save money, to try to keep my reason and call my soul my own. The strain of pity and sadness was so deep that I followed the plan of habit, having lost all sense of right or wrong, whether to go or to stay. Alas, painful situations stifle feeling and loving until one is numb in one's heart and there is nothing left to give or to take. These times of despair and self-hatred are 'when a fella needs a friend'. Best of all, a listener. Nothing relieves the pain in one's heart more than to tell it. If you tell a doctor where the pain is in your body, for a fee he will try to heal you. But who is there to heal your guilt, conflict and defeat? God, you will say. Yes, if you feel His presence and know that He is your listener.

Sir Malcolm Sargent was such a believer, and held the key to 'the house of many mansions'. This made him a great conductor of choral and religious works. To hear him conduct the *Messiah*, *Gerontius*, *Death and Transfiguration* and *The Kingdom* was to be wrung out with the beauty and agony of the performance. Having the human touch, his choirs would sing as they had never sung before, so inspired and stirred were they by their maestro. Malcolm and his music became the key to happiness now and always through a trust that I will leave when my sun sets. Malcolm became my trustee to seek and find the gifted, the talented of any creed or colour and give them the chance to study and be heard. It will be a modest fund, but better to discover only one who should be heard, than no one at all.

It usually took me several weeks to get my house physically

and morally in order each time I came back from the wars. I would try to pick up where I had left off, which is not easy in a social life, the only kind of life I had, if you can call it a life, as I never stayed put long enough to grow. The constant stream of unhappy letters from mother that slid under my door at least three times a week knocked the sun out of my sky; but she was my mother and I loved her deeply. The loneliest kind of loving in all the world.

During one of these unhappy American visits, I met a young publisher at a party, who asked me to lunch with him the following day, saying that he had a proposition to make to me. He asked me to write the story of my life, and said that his company wanted to publish it. He promptly made me an offer, giving me a contract, which, alas, I didn't sign. I asked him if he were feeling all right, because I had no story to tell . . . no story to sell. He said that he was feeling quite well thank you, so here it is!

Certainly not a success story, not even a ducal one. I wear a tarnished hollow crown and have been made only too aware of my unimportance. I have tried to live with it, more in theory than in practice, for I am too vulnerable, unsure of myself and my welcome. I think that I have carried it off with some style, but after that I haven't got what it takes.

I was supplied with three different collaborators, an American and two British, for I had never written anything in my life, and hadn't a clue how to begin. However, I was too self-conscious and shy to work with anyone. Then another publisher friend said to me, 'You can do it yourself.' I went out the following day and bought a typewriter, and with two fingers, for I know no more how to type than I do to write, I have beaten out this saga, for what it's worth. My friend said, 'Get it all out and down. Let it rip.' I have done, in my mid-Atlantic jargon.

During the many winters I came to be with mother, I used to stay at the Westbury, and I will always remember one early evening during a three day blizzard, a snowdrift as big as a house.

I love a snowstorm. I mean the real thing—a blizzard, when it snows and blows for two days and two nights, and drifts become higher than the tallest man.

I was in such a storm in New York City that winter, and delighted in walking in the tiny flakes that turned me completely white in an instant. How snow sparkles and crunches and quiets all sound. That great and noisy city was still and quite silent. Skis and sledges replaced the motor cars that were lost under drifts. It was rather fun to poke one's hand carefully into a mound and find a Cadillac. With all means of travel utterly paralysed, most people cursed the snow—but there was one little girl who blessed it. . . .

While I was sitting reading in my hotel room at about four o'clock in the afternoon, the first day after the storm had ended, I heard a terrific thud. I thought, that's a jolly big snowdrift falling off the roof—as they often do when it begins to melt. Then I heard a whimper, then a moaning, so I went to the window overlooking the glass domed court ten floors below to see where the sounds were coming from. Many other people came to their windows also, for they too had heard the mighty fall and the little cries. To my horror, I saw a dark haired little girl in a party frock lying on her back in a great white snowdrift—on top of the glass dome! She stirred a little and whimpered again, and everyone rushed to get help, for no one could reach her, except from below. It was freezing again and the child was cold, frightened and broken—there was much blood on the snow. Very soon the ambulance siren could be heard, and quickly it arrived. The skilled hands gently lifted the girl on to the stretcher and took her away.

Sixteen floors, sixteen floors she had fallen, and lived! Believe it or not, she still lives, and will mend—only because of a snowdrift.

I felt so happy having chosen Malcolm Sargent to be my trustee for my trust fund, and thankful to him for accepting. He had such a talent for discovering the gifted and giving them the chance to be heard. For instance, James Milligan, the tall,

young, good-looking Canadian, the perfect Wotan! Before he
was given the part at Covent Garden, he sang Wotan in
Europe, where he received ovations after every performance.
Why were they so slow to recognize this artist in England, for
when they finally did, he had a heart attack in Beirut and died,
still in his early thirties; he never once sang Wotan at Covent
Garden.

Malcolm also found Kathleen Ferrier, the lovely young
contralto who was as beautiful to look at as she was to hear.
She too was stricken at the height of her career with cancer,
and her rich, warm, compassionate song was stilled forever.

Then Malcolm! I saw it in his eyes the night we were
dining in his flat after a concert in the Albert Hall. Never more
than six or eight were invited to dine with the maestro after
every performance, especially during the Proms. What fun
these evenings were, indeed a way of life. Malcolm needed to
unwind, and surrounded himself with his close friends to do
just that, with good talk and laughter, usually until one o'clock
in the morning.

Before he settled for after-Prom suppers in his flat in Albert
Hall Mansions, he used to take his guests to the Savoy Grill.
He enjoyed his special table and the stir his arrival caused.
Many times I went there with him and became a part of the
pantomime. Other nights, when there was no concert, he
would often dine at the Garrick Club. One night when he was
taking me to the theatre, we dined there; as we had too little
time, we rushed through our meal, and after it, in fun, I
gasped for breath. Malcolm was not amused. He said, 'St-e-a-dy
. . . remember who you are!' He never missed a look, a move
or a pretty face. Indeed, if mine had not pleased him, I doubt
if we would have got further than the first time we met at a
luncheon at the Dorchester at the end of the war. He was in
fine feather then and, as always, dominated the conversation,
or should one say talk? I don't think that there were many
who held a real conversation with Malcolm, or knew what
was at the back of his mind.

Many times I was his guest, one of the lucky ones, and

delighted in my good fortune. We called it 'The Club', for one really had to become a member of his world of music to be asked more than once or twice. I met so many fascinating people and artists. We both loved the elegant, pomp and circumstance, and crowned heads. There were plenty of those there, but there were others too who bore, or had borne great responsibility for their country. These were the cosy evenings that we loved best.

His guests for supper always preceded him to his flat next door to the Albert Hall, though he did take one of us in his car, which had to drive round the block after every performance. It was quite a stunt, this get-away. Each time he took me with him I was glad when it was over, in case the car was overturned or the windows broken by the Promenaders who loved him and wanted to tell him so. When we arrived at his flat, the first to greet him was Hughie, his white budgerigar, who would fly from the top of his cage with a squeak of joy to greet his beloved maestro, and perch upon his head or shoulder.

The night I saw the fear in his eyes was during supper after a concert. The Norwegian Ambassador and his wife were there, Malcolm's god-daughter, Lilius Sheepshanks, Lord Boothby and myself. Malcolm was not eating well. Not that he ever did eat very much, but this night, not at all. Sylvia Darley, his devoted head secretary (he had three secretaries) looked worried, very unusual for enigmatic Sylvia, who never showed her feelings.

Malcolm then admitted that he had suffered some mysterious pain; it had been diagnosed as gall bladder trouble, and he was going that very night to a nursing home. He was preoccupied, even though he tried to be his usual gay and amusing self. That night at two o'clock he went to hospital. He was operated on, and he and we were told that nothing malignant had been found, that he would soon recover and be on his way to Australia to conduct his engagements there, which he did. This was just before Christmas.

The following summer when I came back from New York, I was asked by the French Ambassador and Madame La Baronne de Courcel to come to an intimate luncheon they were giving for Malcolm in the presentation of the Légion d'Honneur. When I got to the embassy, that loveliest of embassies in Kensington Gardens, spreading over lawns into Hyde Park, I gasped when I saw Malcolm. I saw it all, and when he took me in his arms to kiss me, I could feel and see the terrible emaciation. He was always slight and slim, but dear God, not like this! Even the sparkle had gone, and when the ambassador made the ceremony of presentation of the order from his government, and kissed Malcolm on both cheeks, I thought I would burst out crying, watching his stricken face. He nearly cried, too, when he had to make his speech of thanks. He, the most amusing, easy speaker and *raconteur*, was finding it hard to find the right words, and looked as though he would drop.

I knew then that all that I had feared was true, and that this truly good and remarkable man would not be with us for very long. He retired from the scene, and made his final appearance at the opening of the Proms. I don't think anyone who saw it will ever forget it. For the entire day before he was given injections of every sort and kind to enable him to rise from his bed, get to the Albert Hall and go out there on the platform which was his real home, to say good-bye to his beloved Promenaders.

It was an act of such courage that only one who believed in God as he did could have got through that macabre, heroic, heartbreaking finale. Thank God I was not in the audience, but like most of us who loved him dearly, I watched on television, and cried as I have seldom cried before. The joy this dear man had given to the world was over for him and for all of us, and like the little bird who lost its mate in *Seadrift*, which Malcolm so often conducted, sang: 'No more . . . no more.'

Not long after his tragic and final appearance at the Proms, knowing he had very little time left to live, 'His Elegance', for that was my name for him, sent for me to come. When I got to the room where he lay, I sat by his bed and tried not to show my distress. He took my hand and tried to comfort me, and told me what to do with the trust after he had gone. Also what to do with the rest of my life, and I felt closer to Malcolm than ever before, as the mantle of his external personality fell away and revealed this adorable man as he really was, soon to be with God.

I watched Hughie, who was sitting on Malcolm's chest. He kept talking to Malcolm and to himself, and seemed to know just how it was and would be. How it loved him and seemed anxious to tell him so. While I sat there listening to Malcolm and knowing that I would never see this gallant and dear friend alive again, it was Malcolm who gave me courage. I gave him nothing at all, except my love. It was a poor return for so many years of happiness that will last me all my life, and can be passed on with its fullness of joy to the whole wide world through our trust fund.

The little bird in *Seadrift* was a sad little bird, but I have found such a happy one in New York of all places. It starts its song in March, and sings with unspeakable sweetness and softness during the night in Central Park. You won't believe this I know, unless you listen very carefully between the hours of one and five in the morning, when the city sleeps. Then you will hear it and hold your breath with disbelief, and in order not to miss a note, for it seems to be singing to itself very *pianissimo*. I remembered from my childhood that blackbirds in America don't sing as they do in England, and there are no nightingales, so what is this brave little bird that I have heard many times over many years? No one that I have told about it can tell me, and I am sure they think that I am queer in the head. But I am not queer in the head, for I have found it and heard it and seen it during the day. I watch it from my hotel window, and can't believe that anything so tiny can ring out such joy just to be alive. In April and May, by night and by day, it sings with great gusto as though its little heart and throat would burst with the song of delight. I have never heard such a song of happiness. Could it be the American Song Sparrow, this little brown chap? I could be wrong, but that is what it looks like to me—and until you have heard its song of the joy of living, you have missed your own reason for being alive.

I had a pigeon with the hiccoughs who came every night to sleep outside my window. It used to wake me up with its 'h-i-i-c' in the middle of the night. I would get out of bed and reach out to lift it round the corner so that it would hic itself to sleep somewhere else. Its other nocturnal noises were the greeting and taking leave of its mate, for these two have slept there together every night for several years. What women will put up with to keep their man! Snoring is bad enough, but hiccoughs is too much! Anyway, this cooing couple were my companions, and I liked knowing that they were there.

Never take a flat on the top floor under the roof, unless you want to freeze in winter, roast in summer and like thunder and lightning to get in bed with you . . . and burglars! Not in bed . . . but almost. Six I've heard on the roof, one of whom went away far richer than when he had come—by two mink coats and a bag full of silver which he dropped in his flight down the fire escape, when a brave little porter shone a torch in his face and frightened him.

The ones I saw were a youth on the roof and his mate on the wall below. This thief was about seventeen years old and carried a flick knife. The night porter caught him by the scruff of the neck and proudly handed him over to the police. The other I saw was also young, slim and fair. Very neat in a dark suit and cap. He stood up there over my head gazing at London in the dusk. Each time I rang down to the porter on duty to tell him about the stealthy visitor that I could hear. Each time the police arrived . . . the thief had vanished . . . Why? because there is a bell that rings out in the night whenever the door to the roof is opened, which of course the police have to do. I watched the whole performance on a Friday night when at ten to one I heard the familiar steps over my head again.

I thought, shall I or shan't I ring down to the porter and tell him? Then I got up to see if I could see anyone . . . and there he was! Young and with a mop of long dark hair . . . but the COAT! He was stuck on the high wire fence between us and the hotel next door. I was fascinated watching him pouring over the fence . . . or trying to . . . in a *maxi*! What a thing to go burgling in! . . . a coat down to your ankles. Well . . . I thought he is certainly with it and was about to say 'How are you doing' . . . when having finally got himself over the fence, he vanished. Within three minutes he began to climb back again!

I'll never forget that dark form slithering over the spiky wire like a black caterpillar. So there he was back with us. I had better tell the night porter, who is Irish. 'Mother o' God' he said 'I'll be after ringin' the police' . . . 'after' is right . . . by the time the police got to the roof with bell ringing out like New Year's Eve the MAXI could be 'after' being half way to Brighton!

In 1969, I was in two minds whether to stay near mother as she seemed frail and was ninety-three years old, or go back to England as usual. In spite of my own misgivings and the doctor's advice to go, I went to work on my story and got through the summer, a season I take no pleasure in at any time unless I can sit in the sea. Mother's letters, now written for her by a nurse, came as frequently as ever, and we telephoned to each other twice a month.

What I did not like was the sense of warning I felt about mother. I wrote to the nurse and the doctor that I was worried, and they wrote back not to worry, that all was well, if slowing down, in the Gold Fish Bowl. Even so, in October I thought that I should return to New York earlier than usual. In November I accepted many invitations, including one royal one, a reception for the Queen Mother at St James' Palace, and another to dine with Prince Georg and Princess Ann of Denmark. It was a lovely invitation, and Ann asked me to wear a tiara. All was got ready and the mood was gay.

Then I got a stranger than usual letter from mother. Almost all of her letters have been full of woe and death. Indeed it had been so for at least thirty years, so one had had to harden one's heart; but this time I felt a cold chill and sent a cable to her doctor, asking how she really was, and whether I should come immediately. Three days passed, and I got no answer. I tried to think that he did not think it necessary to cable and was writing, but I didn't believe it, so I cabled again, reply paid. I also cabled Tommy Emmet, asking if he would find out if it were the usual cry of wolf, or whether I should come at once. Those were the three longest days of my life. I finally received a cable from the doctor, telling me that mother's deterioration was very slow, with little or no change since I had left in late May, and that there was a nurse by the telephone who would give me any details, but there was no need for me to come.

I rang, and got a nurse unknown to me, who kept on asking who I was and to hang on until she could wake mother up and get her to the telephone. Then I heard mother say: 'Tell my daughter to come after Christmas.' Then I knew that something awful was wrong, but not final. I then got a cable from Tommy saying that he was in touch with the doctor and would ring me.

The following morning at nine o'clock, the telephone rang, and there was Tommy. 'It's all over,' he said. I didn't know what he meant, and asked what was all over. Then he told me that my tiny, exquisite, wilful little mother had gone to God. My small bedroom is still full of that message, and the familiar sounds of the pigeons and blackbirds don't change a thing. I will never forget those words as long as I remain behind on earth, or be able to live with them and the terrible guilt that is mine.

I sat dazed by the telephone thinking it would ring again, and I would be told that it was all a hideous mistake and that it would be mother telling me so. It did ring again, and a man's voice asked me to dine. To this day I don't know who it was or what else he said. I just hung up, saying over and over to myself: 'I have no one, no one in all the world, please take me too.' Even though it was too late, I wanted to get to her as soon as possible.

Lord Kildare, my former step-son Gerald, had already booked my flight in a VC10 for a few days hence. He is a director of the Piper Aircraft, and greases the wheels whenever I fly. He is also a very human, kind man and a good friend to me. As soon as I could make any sense, I rang Gerald and told him. I was in such a state of shock that I didn't feel anything except the urgency to get to New York. How sympathetic and understanding he was. I will never forget his kindness when I needed it most. 'You will come with me on Saturday,' he said. 'I will change your flight, and we will go together.' No one could have been more considerate and unselfish. I was so touched and grateful to him; because of him I was able to pull myself together enough to start packing up my flat. Funnily enough, I had already packed two of my three cases, having a sort of premonition of urgency. I had twenty-four hours to shut up shop, cancel my engagements and be ready at nine o'clock on Saturday morning, when Denis FitzGerald, Leinster's cousin, would pick me up in his car and take me to the airport where Gerald would be waiting. The few friends who had to be told of my loss were most helpful and kind, but my in-laws, Gerald and Denis, were quite wonderful, bless them.

I have been alone so much and been through so much alone, that I don't know what I would have done without these two, especially Gerald. I suppose I would have got through somehow, but thank God for such a kind stepson . . . and an ex at that!

When we were airborne, Gerald went up to the cockpit at the invitation of the captain, and took the controls. He is a pilot himself, and he enjoyed 'the feel' of the superb VC10. While he was flying us through sunny skies at at least thirty-eight thousand feet, the captain, who had obviously been told about my loss, came back to sit with me. Not only did he try to keep my mind off my sorrow, but he asked me to come up to the cockpit too.

Now this is something I have always wanted to do. Being, as you well know, the apprehensive type, and afraid of take-offs and landings, I thought if I could watch it all happening from the front seat of the aircraft with the officers and crew, I would

learn a lot and lose some of my fear. So when the captain
invited me to go forward with him, I jumped at this welcome
chance. Gerald came back to our seats, and I went up with the
captain. I couldn't get over how small it was, and with only
three men to run the whole show. And the instruments—
millions of them! Some making little ticking noises, some
flashing wee lights of red, green, red, green and nobody seemed
to be doing anything. They put me into a small seat and put
earphones on my head. How kind they were being to a lady
with a hole in her heart! The jargon over the earphones was
all Greek to me, but I was so happy to be where I was, and felt
myself growing braver every minute. When I thought that I
might outstay my welcome, I went back to my seat. But the
best part was to come. When we were due to come in at
Kennedy Airport, the captain came back again and asked me
if I would like to 'bring her in'. This was really exciting!

I was put back into the same seat, and I wouldn't have
missed this part of the journey for all the tea in China. Three
times our runway was changed, and the quiet up front was
complete, except for the earphones. All was concentration.
Even I was silent. I couldn't understand any of the talk-down
language, but I was fascinated. Each time we got low enough
to come in, we were guided by lights flicking along hedges
and fields like dashes and lines.

The lights really talked. Even I could understand them. Tick,
tick, tick, they would go, and we would follow. Twice we had
to wait and change. Then we were on the home stretch. My
heart beat so hard and fast I thought it would burst with the
excitement. The skill and the silence! Good heavens, I had no
idea that it was as simple and complicated as this! When we
touched down, even I didn't know. It was like thistledown. I
can't think that I will ever be frightened again—certainly not
if I fly with that crew. Well, that's what I told myself at the
time, but just show me a plane, and another way to go, and
I'll take it—the other way!

When we arrived at Kennedy Airport, we were swept
through Customs, and Gerald and I parted. Dear Tommy was

waiting for me, and took me and my grief and guilt into his keeping. He arranged everything, while I sat stunned in a state of shock and tried to sort out the millions of pieces of paper in mother's flat to find out her wishes. The lawyer had no instructions except what was in her will. I was so undone that I could not face anyone except Tommy. He arranged the lonely little service at Campbells, and the music, got the flowers, notified the few who cared, and prepared it all with such loving kindness. When the last farewell came and the lovely baritone voice sang 'God be in my head . . .', all my will to live died with her.

What do you do when the money stops and you are given fifteen months by the State to pay death duties, and the only way you can pay is to sell the third of the Brooklyn property you inherited—and nobody wants to buy the third?

What do you do when all the debts and losses you tried so hard to stop while she lived become a nightmare of reality—and it's all yours?

What do you do when the few she trusted and believed would be loyal and helpful, turn out to be the users and abusers you always knew them to be, and they all come down upon you like a ton of bricks?

So, I went to Sweden! Yes, it's good to get up and go when you are black and blue and sorry for yourself. The British Ambassador, Sir Archibald Ross, and his gay, pretty wife, Mary, with whom I had stayed when they were *en poste* in Portugal, had asked me to come for Whitsun to my surprise and delight, for my visit to Lisbon shook the embassy there when I slept in the attic—by choice! So back I flew to London to leave my luggage and repack and go on to Stockholm.

It was a visit that I wouldn't have missed for anything, with all the warmth of heart and hearth that I sadly needed. Such a comfortable embassy, right on the lake; the sun smiled upon us the entire week, even at night! I wouldn't have believed that one could hear and see people out in boats sunning themselves at two thirty in the morning. There just isn't any long real night, or wasn't in May, and I found this so exciting that I spent most of the so-called night hanging out of the window watching this phenomenon. I delighted in everything I saw and did while I was there, and I was told that I was lucky in the weather. It was about time that I was lucky in something, so I made the most of it.

Archie drove us many miles and showed us many interesting places and things. It reminded me of Canada, with its clear light and miles and miles of open stretches of country and trees and lakes—millions of them. I never saw so many lakes in all my life; far more than those in Canada. No matter how far or where you looked, there was another sparkling blue lake. How I loved it all! The houses were lovely and warm, and so comfortable, with beautiful furniture and decorated with taste and style.

We dined one night at Countess Bernadotte's, the American widow of Count Bernadotte, nephew of the king. During the war, I had met her and her husband at an enormous official luncheon given for them at the Waldorf Astoria in New York. I had the pleasure of sitting next to Count Bernadotte, and found him warm, tolerant and compassionate. Indeed, both he and his lovely wife seemed to possess these qualities, and there was a feeling of peace and contentment about them. Remembering that I had known her husband, Countess Bernadotte took me into another room away from the guests to show me his portrait. It was a framed life-sized photograph hanging over the mantelpiece. I had never seen anything like this before, and I must say it startled me, because it was so alive and I felt he too was there. She lives alone there, much loved by the people. There were about twenty of us for dinner, which was given for Archie and Mary. A few Swedish customs, such as not drinking until the hostess drinks, toasting your neighbour with '*Skol*', a speech to the guest of honour, and his or her reply, were in use, but the one I found utterly charming came immediately after dinner.

I noticed that everyone was going up to the hostess as we left the dining-room, and shaking her by the hand, thanking her for a delicious dinner. I thought, Good Lord, they are all going home, and we haven't had our coffee yet! So I watched to see what Archie and Mary did, and they too shook hands with Countess Bernadotte, and so did I—and nobody went home until two! Apparently the later you stay the more flattering it is to your hostess. Well, it was a lovely party, but my good manners would not stand up to proving my pleasure every night in the week, even if there isn't any night!

My first summer in London, with mother no longer my guiding star was something I couldn't get used to or accept, and I still can't. To me she is still there in Park Avenue waiting for me to come back. None of it is real or makes sense, and I am amazed at how generous she was to me on so little money. For I am her heir and executrix, and now I know, as I know the reckoning. It was good to try to keep going and not to brood alone, so I was thankful to those who kindly asked me to dinners and parties. It may be only the icing on the cake, but it takes you out of yourself—especially Paul Getty, who was sitting next to me one night at dinner and asked me how I managed my money! I was so flattered by this compliment that I warmed to him at once and liked this solemn looking shy tycoon with all the social graces of a prince. He seems to enjoy his pleasures like a small boy with a secret as he smiles to himself. What do you think he had for lunch the other day at Sutton Place? Shredded wheat! I watched as I ate more than my share of roast beef. So that's what keeps the richest man rich . . . all those wheaties! But those who put me right back into myself were two monologuists—an American Ambassador and a British Prime Minister! They talked at me until I was completely Bla-a-a, and when I changed places with another, they kept right on talking and never noticed! Brother, could they talk!

When it took eleven American men to get one American woman down, and all over a sale of a small corner of Brooklyn . . . or was it only one who was my Judas? Well I learned one thing, an American may not walk, talk or wear his clothes with style . . . but never underestimate him when he is your lawyer and in the driver's seat . . . Fasten your seat belt!

All said and done, as I walk along looking at my thoughts, I feel a great surge of warmth fill my heart for this green and pleasant land, and long to strike roots and call it home. I wish 'My Imp' had been less of an Imp and that I had been born to the life I got and went out to get, in my wonderful dream world of Disney. I went forth with stars in my eyes and my heart on both sleeves, rejoicing in the pomp and circumstance of dear England, trying to be the heroine of my life and not its victim. I wanted the goodwill of many, the affection of a few, and the love of one. Well, it's not the end of the road, so give me the birds and the bees in a green place with a cosy someone to laugh with. There dwells the sweetness of life. So let us end this saga with a far cry from Brooklyn of 'What Price Duchess?' . . . and make tomorrow sing.

© C.M.Wrigley